MW01228601

Direct Your Letter to the Matador Ranch

A Cowboy's Long Distance Romance with a Cotton Farmer's Daughter

Marisue Burleson Potts

Direct Your Letter to the Matador Ranch
A Cowboy's Long Distance Romance with a Cotton Farmer's Daughter
Marisue Burleson Potts © 2022

Photo Credit for About the Author: Julie Childs
Book Production by Aloha Publishing, AlohaPublishing.com
Editor: Jennifer Regner

Hardcover ISBN: 978-1-7356605-8-5
Softcover ISBN: 978-1-7356605-5-4
eBook ISBN: 978-1-7356605-6-1

Published by Mollie Burleson Ranch Ltd.

Printed in the United States of America

Dedication

With respect and awe, I dedicate this book to the extended Kieth/Keith family for their preservation of the history of Motley County, Texas, with letters, photographs, stories, hard work, and perseverance through the lean years to celebrate the bountiful ones.

Contents

Preface

A marriage of two cultures in Texas
The true story of D.C. Kieth and Ella E. Cribbs
as told in their personal letters

One of the first marriages in Motley County was that of a Matador cowboy, D.C. Kieth, and a cotton farmer's daughter, Ella E. Cribbs. The ceremony in Matador, Texas, ended a long-distance correspondence that began five years earlier in 1886.

This marriage of two cultures is revealed in their correspondence, a collection of letters that was found in an old shoebox in the home of Charlie Keith, their youngest son. D.C. Kieth's and Ella E. Cribbs' letters were postmarked from the river bend cotton country of Ft. Spunky, a post office located on the Brazos River, and the cattle country's vanguards of Dockum Ranch, Tee Pee City, Matador, Jayton, Estacado, Della Plains, and "Floid" (Floyd) City. Many of those post offices existed for only a few years and their locations are now marked with Texas Historical Commission markers.

Miss Cribbs, who described herself as hardier than looks might suppose, bragged that she picked 6,000 pounds of cotton in the fall of 1888. However she longed for the last bale to be picked before Christmas, so she and her sister could "have a lively time." Her braggadocio turned to despair when she realized her father planned to plant an even bigger crop the following year. The young woman, who was bordering on spinsterhood at age 23, assumed a very important economic role in the family as an unpaid field laborer and household helper.

The long-distance romance began when D.C. Kieth obtained Ella Cribbs' name from a fellow cowboy and "cold-wrote" her a letter, asking to correspond with her. He described cow hunts, night herding, trips up the trail to Chicago, burning of fire guards on the vast plains of the Matador Ranch's pasture, revelry at Tee Pee City, and enduring a lonely post at Christmas time to her in many letters. As the correspondence continued, Kieth attempted to define his ambitions to a woman to whom he had proposed before he had seen her or even learned her age.

The Kieth and Cribbs letters provide a rare opportunity to participate in the flowering of a budding romance, the settling up of cattle country in the ranges of the Dockum, Espuela, and Matador Ranches, and the marriage of the cotton and cowboy cultures in the Texas Rolling Plains.

Letters in a Shoebox, Tied With Twine

When Charlie and Viola Keith, then in their late 80s, embarked on a massive homestead cleaning in 1992, they presented a variety of historical items to the Motley County Museum in Matador, Texas. From storage in their former chicken house, they brought forth a pre-electric pump-style vacuum cleaner, a New Home treadle sewing machine, a kitchen salt box made of wood and hinged with leather, and other items of historical value to the volunteer-run historical museum.

From his pioneer Kieth (the traditional spelling) family's considerable accumulation, Mr. Charlie Keith shared many photographs,
documents and items relating to the early history of Motley County,
Texas. Several items of interest relating to his parents, D.C. and
Ella Cribbs Kieth, included their wedding photograph, her wedding
dress, and the framed certificate of their marriage—the second one
recorded in Motley County, soon after its organization in 1891.

Charlie's smiling wife, Mrs. Viola Keith, brought a tattered
cardboard shoebox tied with frayed twine into the Motley County
Museum lobby. Inside was a collection of 85 letters[1] that D.C. and
Ella had written to each other during their pen-pal courtship of five
years. Nearly all were hand-cancelled and dated, with some posted
from places such as Dockum's Ranch, Tee Pee City, and Estacado,
which existed for only a short time in Texas before quietly receding
into history. Through their letters, the couple revealed fragments
of information about themselves and also provided details of their
lives, she on the farming frontier and he on the ranching frontier, as
they progressed toward a marriage of the two cultures.

Ella Cribbs, the lovely daughter of the Brazos River cotton culture, was somewhat coerced into writing to the Tennessee plowboy-
turned Texas cowboy, D.C. Kieth. After five years of exchanging
letters, however, she would pledge her troth to a man she had seen
only once, during a six-day visit. The letters provide personal insight
into the push-pull factors of those drawn to the ever-changing edge
of civilization, one of hardship and adventure, despair and excite-
ment, resolution and hope.

---

1. "Ella Cribbs and D.C. Kieth Letters," Keith Family Collection, Motley County
Historical Museum, Matador, Texas, 79244.

The Cattle Frontier

Daniel Crawford Kieth Sr. was lured from the scenic waterfalls and hills of Franklin County, Tennessee, to look for opportunity in the cattle frontier in Parker County, Texas. In the 1850s, settlers were attracted to the cheap land of gently rolling plains, rich vegetation, and streams and valleys along the Brazos River. Up until the 1840s, the area had been the stronghold of Kiowa and Comanche tribes. The Republic of Texas (1836-1846) had recently been annexed as the state of Texas by the United States, and immigration was being encouraged. Kieth's wife, Susan Bledsoe, birthed their daughter, Sophronia Elizabeth, on 7 October 1855, the year Parker County was organized in Texas with Weatherford as the county seat. The fledgling settlers, led by Isaac Parker, were often harassed by Indian raids.

The threat of Indian raids chased the Kieth family back to Tennessee in time for Daniel Sr. to become involved in the war between the states—the Civil War. Joining Turney's 1st Tennessee Infantry at Winchester, Tennessee, Daniel marched off to Winchester, Virginia, leaving behind his pregnant wife, Susan, and their two children. A large number of Confederates were bivouacked at Camp Jones, Virginia, in crowded and unsanitary conditions that created conditions rife for disease. Daniel Sr. soon took measles, had a relapse, and died of pneumonia, leaving nothing but a letter for his future namesake and the unborn baby's two siblings, Sophronia Elizabeth and Charles Bledsoe Kieth.

D.C. Kieth Sr. (circa 1861)

The following is the letter written by Daniel Crawford Kieth to his children just one month before he departed this life. At the time the letter was written, there were two children, Sophronia and Charles. The third child was born in October 1861, just two months after Daniel Crawford Kieth died of pneumonia. The wife [Susan Bledsoe Kieth] named the new baby after his father whom he would never see: Daniel Crawford Kieth Jr.

Since it has been the will of the All-Wise Ruler of all things who rules our destinies, to call from our midst an esteemed friend in a foreign land whilst he was serving his country as a soldier, we deeply sympathize with his family knowing they have sustained a great loss and humbly trust that those dear orphan children for whom he expressed such love may be reared and trained in the course marked for them in the letter. (Introduction by author unknown.)

[Source: Keith Family Collection, Motley County Museum, Matador, Texas.]

Sgt. Daniel C. Kieth (Keith)

Turney's 1st Tennessee Infantry

Camp Jones, Winchester, Virginia

A Father's Letter

Winchester, Virginia

July 8th, 1861

My Dear Children,

I seat myself to write you a letter, although I know you cannot read it, but you have a mother that can read it. My dear and lovely children, I am a distance of about nine hundred miles from you, in the Confederate Army, for the purpose of defending the rights of you and your mother and all other good Southern people.

Now, my dear children, I will write this as plain as I can, in order that you may be enabled to read it in years to come, provided that I should never return home. My dear children, I hope and trust in God, all through his good mercies I may be permitted to return home to provide a living for you and your mother, and to spend my days on earth with you, and if I never should see you again on earth, I hope to meet you all in Heaven, where we may know each other and enjoy the rich blessing of Heaven, throughout all eternity.

Now my dear children, you have a good and affectionate and kind mother. I want you to obey her in all her commands. I know she will not teach you any evil thing. Never forget the trouble she has seen with you in your infancy, which is at the present time. Keep good company, Always be on your guard when talking and *acting. Never put yourselves in a grown man or woman's place until you are worthy both in age and manners.*

Now, my dear children, this is the advice of a loving father. I hope you will observe and obey it. I subscribe myself as your true and loving father.

s/ Daniel C. Kieth (Keith)

By 1880, the U.S. military had subdued the Indians, and Texas once again beckoned to the Tennessee family. Texas-born Sophronia and her husband, Henry Zachary Taylor Garner, along with Sophronia's brother, 19-year-old D.C. Kieth Jr., headed to the Cross Timbers of Jack County, where Jacksboro served as the county seat.

A year earlier, brothers John and Charles Hensley along with L.A. Wilson served as the vanguard of many small operators who wanted to capitalize on the cattle grazing on free range in the Texas Rolling Plains and breaks of the Brazos and Trinity Rivers. Cattlemen like Charles Goodnight and John Loving gathered herds and blazed trails to burgeoning cattle markets in the north.

D.C. joined his uncle, Jones Kieth of Erath County, in trailing a herd of cattle west, terminating their drive in sparsely settled Dickens County where only 28 people were rustled up for the 1880 census.[2] Just six years after the conclusion of the Red River War of 1874, Kieth camped at the landmark butte Soldier Mound,[3] a fortified

2. *Dickens County: Its Land and People* (Spur, Texas: Dickens County Historical Commission, 1986), p. 386.
3. "Soldier Mound," *The New Handbook of Texas*, Vol. 5. (Austin, Texas: Texas State Historical Association, 1996.), p. 1139.

supply point used by Colonel Ranald S. Mackenzie's troops in their campaign against the Comanches.

The scattering of Indians not yet relocated on the reservations in Indian Territory caused concern for the few settlers scattered in isolated dugouts. Despite the threat and the remoteness, Kieth took a liking to the country dotted by wild mustangs and antelope, and two years later he was there to stay.

As cattlemen scattered their herds, they observed that the short-grass prairie was littered with the bones from herds of buffalo wantonly slaughtered by ambitious hunters and marksmen such as Frank Collinson and W.C. Dockum.[4] When Dockum carved his first dugout into a clay bank, it measured 12 x 14 feet, had a dirt floor, a roof made of buffalo hide, a table made from a dry goods box, seats from powder cans of various colors, depending upon the grade of gun powder, and a bed made with thongs cut from buffalo hide. To serve other buffalo hunters and isolated settlers, he later built what his daughter Grace recalled was a more pretentious dugout for his store that served people up to 100 miles away.[5] A post office was established by 1878, where Kieth's letters were postmarked "Dockum's Ranch," amid revelry created by lonesome cowboys who gathered for fellowship and the musical talents of the genteel Mrs. Dockum.

Bear and panther tracks testified to a presence often unseen but keenly felt. The sense of danger was heightened by the threat of Indian depredations from renegades absent without leave from

4. Collinson, Frank. *Life in the Saddle* (Norman: University of Oklahoma, 1963), p. 57. Also, W.R. Stafford, Nov. 29, 1929, abstract of oral history tape on W.C. Dockum, Espuela Ranch Files, Southwest Collection, Texas Tech University.

5. Dockum, Grace. Oral history, recorded by Ted's Recording Studio, October 1952. Transcript in Motley County Historical Museum, Matador, Texas.

Indian Territory. During 1883 when Kieth returned from a visit to Jack County to his work as a "cow boy," the kidnapping of a 15-year-old boy was reported in what was to be the last Indian scare in Dickens County.[6]

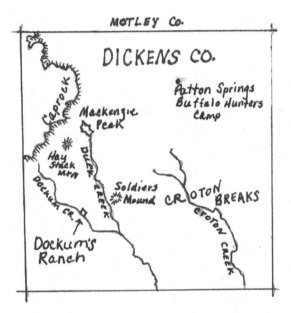

DOCKUM'S RANCH STORE AND POST OFFICE

DICKENS COUNTY, TEXAS

Map of Dockum's Ranch in Dickens County, Texas

The closing of the free-range period loomed with the advancement of surveyors in 1877. Cheap state and railroad land became available for purchase by individuals or foreign-owned corporations, closing the open range by deed, lease, or barbed-wire fencing. At one point, Kieth's intentions seemed to be to return to the farming frontier. Although he believed that he could earn more in cattle

6. *Dickens County: Its Land and People* (Spur, Texas: Dickens County Historical Commission, 1986), p. 386.

country than as a farm laborer, there were drawbacks. The basic pay scale for a cowboy was $30 a month with "board," which sometimes meant meals at the chuckwagon with a bedroll under the stars on the prairie. When the seasonal work slacked off, the men were often laid off or offered onerous jobs of fencing or tank building at the reduced rate of $20 a month.

A group of cowboys, frustrated by low wages and working conditions, became involved in a classic dispute between labor and management with the Cowboy Strike of 1883. Protests from hired hands erupted on ranches in the Panhandle of Texas, resulting in a blacklisting of participants. If the news reached Kieth at Dockum's Ranch of the Cowboy Strike, he did not acknowledge it in his letters. By 1885, the Espuela Cattle Company had bought out 61 small range claims, including Dockum's Ranch, along with Dockum's store merchandise that was moved to the ranch commissary.[7]

Financiers A.M. Britton and S.W. Lomax, at the behest of cattleman H.H. Campbell, became instrumental in establishing the Matador Cattle Company. For profit, the financiers turned it into the Matador Land & Cattle Company, Ltd., with foreign financing by a Scottish syndicate. Likewise, investors absorbed John Hall's Spur Ranch to be reorganized as the Espuela Cattle Company, and then later as the Espuela Land and Cattle Company, Ltd., a British syndicate. The number of cattle at the time of the transfer was estimated to be 40,000.

The drought of 1886 and the weather extremes that followed, coupled with a drop in cattle prices, created hard times for cattlemen and their employees. Kieth could accumulate neither capital nor

---

7. Holden, William Curry. *The Espuela Land & Cattle Company, a Study of a Foreign-Owned Ranch in Texas* (Austin: Texas State Historical Association, 1970), p. 54.

time off working for Dockum's or later for the Espuela. As David Dary pointed out in *Cowboy Culture*,[8] many young men were hit by disillusionment, wanderlust, or homesickness, with only three percent staying longer than five seasons as a cowboy. Looking for an outfit that would allow him the opportunity to run a few cattle, Kieth went to work briefly for TO Ranch, but then for a better wage hired on with the Matador Ranch. The punitive ripple effect, from the Cowboys' Strike of 1883[9] by Panhandle ranch hands for higher wages and better working conditions, reached the ranch management of the JA, the Matador, and the Espuela ranches, when respective managers Charles Goodnight, H.H. Campbell, and S.W. Lomax made an agreement not to allow hands to brand mavericks for their own, and to enforce prohibition and blackball any hand discharged for stealing or drunkenness. The wages remained the same for the common cowboy, about $30 a month during the season of cow work.

In the meantime, Kieth's chores as a cowhand ranged from going on a "cow hunt" to riding night herd, from gathering to branding, from trailing to shipping, and from cleaning out tanks to dragging fire guards. Trail work he considered the hardest chore, but trailing and shipping cattle paid more. The most dangerous job, according to Kieth, was turning the tick-infested herds coming from South Texas, a task that could get a fellow killed by armed drovers intent on trespassing for grass or water for their cattle bound for northern markets.

"Cow hunting on the outside" meant working among other outfits as a "rep," representing the interests of the Espuela. While

8. Dary, David. *Cowboy Culture* (Lawrence: University of Kansas, 1989), pp. 276, 296.
9. "Cowboy Strike of 1883," *The New Handbook of Texas*, Vol. 2 (Austin, Texas: The Texas State Historical Association, 1996), pp. 378, 379.

working for the TO Ranch, he explained that on a cow hunt, he often had to ride all day and, along with 10 or 12 others, guard the cattle at night. While working for the Matador Ranch, however, Kieth's description of a cow hunt fits Dr. W.C. Holden's definition of "still hunting." A single hand, living at a batch camp by himself or with a few others, would ride the range looking for calves to brand during the work lull caused by either the extremely hot summer or cold winter weather.[10]

Duff Green, in writing about the ranches and cowboys in the counties of Dickens, Motley, and Kent, stated that most large outfits had two crews consisting of the branding and trail outfits. The branding outfit stayed on the home range and employed 15 to 20 men, including the boss, cook, and horse wrangler. When a herd was gathered for shipment, the trail men, numbering from a few cowboys up to 11, started for a shipping point of delivery. By the time they returned, a second herd was ready to be delivered.[11] D.C. Kieth evidently had a knack for getting the cattle to shipping points in good shape, because for over 40 years he shipped cattle for the Matadors, traveling as far away as Canada.

---

10. Holden, William Curry. *The Espuela Land and Cattle Company, a Study of a Foreign-Owned Ranch in Texas* (Austin, Texas: Texas State Historical Association, 1970), p. 119.

11. Green, Duff. *Recollections* (Mineral Wells, Texas: Joan Green Lawrence, 1988), p. 233.

The Cotton Frontier

Coming from Tuscaloosa, Alabama, Ella Eugenia Cribbs settled with her family in the isolated river bend community east of the Brazos River and about three miles north of George's Creek, along what historian Rupert Richardson defined as the *farmers' frontier* that ran east from the cattleman's frontier of some 30 to 150 miles.[12]

The Cribbs family's landing place was a settlement first known as Barnardville, a fortified trading post serving the Tonkawas, a peaceable, agricultural tribe which traveled a well-defined trail to the post along a prominent butte. Comanche Peak was known for its use by nomadic Comanches as a lookout, rallying point, and ceremonial site. When the U.S. government removed the Indians to Fort Belknap in the mid-1850s, the diminished Indian barter trade no longer justified the post. The store was moved a mile south to serve settlers. Because of the locals' pugnacious demeanor whenever they assembled, the settlement and post office

---

12. Pool, William C. *A Historical Atlas of Texas* (Austin: Encino Press, 1975), pp. 113-115.

became known as Fort Spunky. As an agricultural trade center, Fort Spunky grew to include a gristmill, blacksmith shop, general store, and feed store.[13] A cotton gin served farmers with hand-picked cotton delivered by mule-drawn wagons. Nearby George's Creek community had frequent revivals with baptisms in the creek and extended revivals conducted by Presbyterian and circuit-riding Methodist preachers.[14]

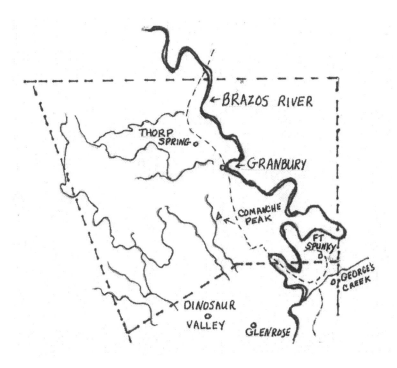

Map of Hood County, Texas

13. Leach, Dorothy. "Fort Spunky, Texas. *The New Handbook of Texas, Vol 2* (Austin, Texas: The Texas State Historical Association, 1996), p. 1118.

14. Granbury Junior Woman's Club. *Hood County History in Picture and Story: 1978.* (Fort Worth: Historical Publishers, 1978).

Settlers like the Cribbs family were drawn to the valleys, breaks, and timber belts of Hood County, where their small farms began to dot what was once prime stock range for horses and cattle. The first raw cotton was brought into the county during the Civil War by W.C. Walters. The need for homespun clothing created such a high demand for his production of four bales that Walters decided to plant a bigger patch on his river farm. His yield of 2,000 pounds of cotton seed was the beginning of cotton planting in the area.[15] For sharecroppers, tenant farmers, and landowners in the river bottoms, cotton became the cash crop and the medium of exchange, with plantings of corn and peanuts serving as secondary crops.

By 1856, about 500 farms of 100 acres each were noted in the county. Four flour and grist mills, nine cotton gins, and 20 common schools served the population of 1,000 county residents. The mail was picked up and delivered two to three times weekly by Concord Coach. Fort Spunky itself boasted of a general store, a gin, a blacksmith shop, and a school with up to 75 pupils.[16] The residents who often gathered for dances and parties found their entertainment in simple pleasures, including religious revivals and spelling matches.

The Cribbs family, composed of Philander and Nannie and children, Maggie, Ella, Dan, and Carrie, lived about a mile from Fort Spunky. An older sister, Lillie, and her husband, Nick Thompson, had formerly lived around Fort Spunky before moving nearer Fort Worth in Tarrant County. A product of the Southern plantation culture, their mother, Nannie McShann, was brought up in Greene County, Alabama, where a slave attended to her every need and even

---

15. Ewell, Thomas. *History of Hood County* (Granbury, Texas: Junior Women's Club, 1956), p. 52.

16. Ewell, Thomas. *History of Hood County* (Granbury, Texas: Junior Women's Club, 1956), pp. 79, 151.

slept in the same room with her. As a young woman of privilege in Tuscaloosa, Nannie was married in 1860 to Philander Cribbs, a "49er." After his gold rush days, Cribbs served as second lieutenant in the 20th Alabama Infantry of the Confederate Army and was twice captured, but paroled each time. With emancipation of the slaves as proclaimed by Abraham Lincoln on January 1, 1863, Nannie found herself practically helpless in a slave-free society and had to be taught by her husband how to perform household chores and cook at the same time that he taught his daughters.[17]

Nannie and Philander Cribbs at their home near Matador, Texas

During Union General William Sherman's devastating march across the South, the Cribbs family's pottery manufacturing plant was burned and destroyed. Because of the difficult days of

17. Traweek, Eleanor. *Of Such as These: A History of Motley County and Its Families* (Quanah, Texas: Nortex Publishers, 1973), p. 223.

Reconstruction following the conclusion of the Civil War, the family left Tuscaloosa for a new start in Texas, a state that had suffered relatively little collateral damage in comparison. Cheap land beckoned, and they settled for a time in Young County, receiving their mail at the post office in Graham, before moving to the Fort Spunky area.

In the emerging but altered cotton culture (sans slaves) in Hood County, Ella was not only willing, but also duty bound, to help her ill and "aging" father and mother, who were considered old and worn out at ages 50 and 45.

Since her sisters were in school, Ella was the chief household helper and caretaker of her ill mother. Ella could clean, scour, cook, sew on a machine, wash, and iron, as well as help with the hog-killing and soap-making. A neighbor once commented, "The Cribbs girls can do anything, commencing with the blackened pot in the kitchen to the finest fancy work."

In a desire to advance her education like her older sister Maggie, Ella expressed a desire to attend Eulogy Bosque at Thorp Springs. When that opportunity for higher education did not materialize, Ella was not too proud to avail herself of an opportunity to attend the local school with much younger students. At age 26, she edged out her younger sister Carrie for the honorary recitation at the end of the term. She also served as an instructor for a penmanship class and for her Sunday school class, but in the latter, thought herself more of a scholar than a teacher. Although she called herself rustic, homely, and not very entertaining, the strikingly handsome young woman added artistic renderings to her envelopes and letters which often contained stanzas of poetry.

No stranger to hard times or the hard work necessary to keep the family farm going, Ella Cribbs found the family's standard of living, their social status, and the type of work she performed, whether household or field, directly linked to the price of cotton. Out of necessity, she and many unmarried daughters and wives of landowners or tenant farmers were often expected to work for the family without compensation. This situation, according to researcher Ruth Allen, provided unfair competition for the low-paid, male wage earner, and also exploited the feminine work force.[18] Allen indicated that in a large part of the agricultural economy of the South, the importance of children as a workforce made women indispensable to the farm, but it also placed them in subordinate positions. In some cases, women were degraded to serving as breeders of a labor supply, or their immediate and future health was compromised by the physically demanding work.

Although she preferred to work in the house, Ella took great pride in her role as fieldworker and bragged about the amount of cotton she could pick: 191 pounds her best day and 6,800 pounds her best season. In the fall of 1889, before their own cotton opened, she picked for other farmers and earned $10.35.[19] A year later, while making a "full hand at home," she again worked outside the home and earned $45.60, spending $10 on herself and the rest on the family. Ella seems to fit into Allen's profile of the "family system of peonage,"[20] whereby an unmarried daughter who lived at home worked in the house and on the farm, often without compensation, and was likely to do some work for hire in a replacement for slave labor, once utilized in the Southern cotton culture.

---

18. Allen, Ruth. *The Labor of Women & Production of Cotton* (Austin, Texas: University of Texas Bulletin #3134, Sept. 8, 1931), pp. 144-145.

19. Cribbs, Ella. Letter of October 4, 1889.

20. Allen, Ruth. *The Labor of Women & Production of Cotton* (Austin, Texas: University of Texas Bulletin #3134, Sept. 8, 1931), p. 147.

A woman picking cotton in the Reconstruction South

"The problem of labor of women in the production of cotton is woven into the warp and woof of the civilization of the Southern cotton economy," Allen wrote in a 1931 University of Texas bulletin. According to Allen's study, the greatest danger to women working in the field, especially girls who were in a formative stage, was from picking cotton because of the stooping, pulling, and lifting required.[21] Ella bragged that she was "hardier than looks might suppose," but sprained her right arm carrying and packing heavy cotton sacks. When she was not picking cotton during the four-month season, she helped her father plant peanuts and 20 acres of corn, hoed corn, and gathered "gubers" [sweet potatoes] on the Brazos bottomland. When it was too hot to work around midday, she wrote letters to her cowboy pen pal in the West. At one point, Ella's fingers and hands were so sore from picking cotton that she complained she had been unable to write to Kieth.

---

21. Allen, Ruth. *The Labor of Women & Production of Cotton* (Austin, Texas: University of Texas Bulletin #3134, Sept. 8, 1931), p. 146.

Mr. Cribbs, like other farmers in the area, was plagued by drought, oversupply, falling prices, and labor shortages. As a means of coping with these problems, the farmers in Hood County formed six lodges of Grangers that flourished for a few years before the Farmer's Alliance took their place, "dividing the solid democracy, though democrats carried the majority."[22] Forming in Texas in 1877, the National Farmer's Alliance had promised to fight falling prices, exorbitant freight rates, the lack of price supports, and other agrarian ills facing drought-stricken farm families.

Ella, along with nine other women, joined the local Farmer's Alliance, a populist, grassroots organization that encouraged farmers to pool resources, form cooperatives, hire or recommend other members for employment, and sell their cotton through an agent.[23] She confessed to Kieth that it was the "only secret society" to which she belonged. Like many other women, Ella seemed attracted to the Farmer's Alliance because of the organization's stand for Prohibition. In her letters she plied Kieth with questions about his stand on the prohibition, to which he replied, "I am high tempered and drink whiskey, but can controle my self."[24] When Ella attended a Prohibition Picnic, she was disappointed that she was not on the winning side of the debate, with the "anti's" claiming victory.

Her father, Philander Cribbs, and others in the highly mobile society looked even further westward to the emerging frontiers for a new start. For three years, Cribbs had been entertaining the idea of uprooting the family to Washington Territory, but the drought situation didn't allow them enough profit to get away. Many young

---

22. Ewell, Thomas. *History of Hood County* (Granbury, Texas: Junior Women's Club, 1956), p. 151.
23. Farmer's Alliance Records, Minutes of Hood County, 187-1896, Microfilm H 776 Hood Co., Southwest Collection, Texas Tech University, Lubbock, Texas.
24. D.C. Kieth letter to Ella Cribbs, February 15, 1888.

men of Hood County, described by Ella as "the life of the country," were leaving for the West.

"Time doesn't seem so hard in Western folks as 'tis with us farmers," she mused. When she decided to marry Kieth and join him in Matador, her father went to check out the possibilities for moving the entire family there. Ill himself, Cribbs at 55 and Nannie, who at 50 was determined to go with the family or die trying, ultimately embarked on a journey in an open wagon that taxed both their resolve and strength. For Ella, she was leaving behind not only the comforting influences of church, community, and social gatherings, but also her chance for further education and the opportunity of earning wages, however meager. Yet, as she explained in her letters to Kieth, she was also abandoning the physical rigors of cotton picking and the agony of a prolonged drought. In the trying economic times, lawlessness in the neighborhood seemed to be increasing, and she was thankful her brother was with Kieth on the open range. In addition, she hoped her family would be less likely to be exposed to the epidemics sweeping through the "sickly" Brazos River country, by going to the higher, drier, less populated country.

La Grippe, so fatal when followed by pneumonia, had claimed eight students in nearby Johnson County in just one week. The illness, accompanied by high fever and chills, had many potential causes. According to researcher C.E.A. Winslow, mild cases of trichinosis, an infestation of roundworm in pork which is transmissible to man, were often diagnosed as "grippe," nephritis, or rheumatic fever. Small, self-sufficient farms often fed hogs garbage, then ate the hogs, perpetuating the cycle of the roundworm. He also theorized that many diseases, such as typhoid fever, scarlet fever, septic sore throat, diphtheria, diarrhea, and intestinal complaints, could be traced directly to milk production with the lack of cleanliness, pasteurization, and refrigeration.[25]

Sickness in the unhealthy river-bottom climate was also promoted by malaria-carrying insects, poor sanitation practices, and tainted water. Dr. George Rohé, in an 1890 textbook on hygiene, cited river water, the carrier of refuse, as a source of "mountain fever," malaria, or typhoid with malarial complications. Other diseases he attributed to impure drinking water were yellow fever, diphtheria, diarrhea, dysentery, cholera, scarlet fever, and roundworm and tapeworm infestations.[26]

In the pioneer era, human waste was *not* commonly known to be a menace to public health. Disease, it was conjectured, was caused by an accumulation of putrid matter, so surface contamination of soil with fecal matter was not considered harmful. However, the most dangerous polluting matter was the excreta of human beings, especially from patients with typhoid or cholera. Outhouses or privies in the garden or yard often contaminated water sources. Rohé advocated the prevention of sanitation diseases by purity of food and water, as well as cleanliness of body, clothing, and dwelling, but either his message was not widely known, or primitive circumstances prevented their implementation.

When Ella's brother, Daniel Cribbs, was exposed to a smallpox epidemic while looking for work in the Houston area, he returned home sick with fever. The neighbors were so fearful of contagion that they would not visit the family. During a visit to the Cribbs farm from their home near Fort Worth in Tarrant County, Ella's older sister Lillie Thompson and her family were exposed to whooping cough. Back home, members of the family became ill, and the

25. Winslow, C.-E. A. *Man and Epidemics* (Princeton: Princeton University Press, 1952), p. 142.

26. Rohé, George H., M.D. *Textbook of Hygiene*, Second Edition (Philadelphia, Pennsylvania: F.A. Davis Publisher, 1890), p. 395.

youngest child died in July of 1891. By October, their doctor had "given up" the eldest child, who succumbed to "Malriah [Malaria], fever & pneumonia."

For the slender hope of something better, Ella was willing to exchange the known hardships for the prospect of a crude, isolated frontier life in a half-dugout. The major lures were cheap land, economic improvement, the possible escape from lawlessness, and a more healthful climate. In the new way of life, cattle, not cotton, was king, a fact that would soon be changed by the invasion of nesters intent on advancing the farming frontier. Eventually, cotton farms would dot the Rolling Plains and the High Southern Plains, and the enclave of cattle country would once again come to the Crossed Timbers and East Texas. The boll weevil would be the instigator for change since the plains were, for the time being, free of the insect's devastation of cotton crops.

Cribbs half dugout near Matador, Texas

The Correspondence

By March 1896, Kieth's name showed up on the payroll of the Espuela Land & Cattle Company. The ranch hand confessed to a friend, Bud Merriman, how lonesome a cowboy gets during the bleak winter months, and he wondered if Bud knew some young lady with whom Kieth might correspond. Merriman came up with a name and address of a young woman who lived in a neighborhood about seven miles from his family's home in Hood County.[27]

When Kieth's brief, tentative letter arrived with the postmark of Dockum Ranch, one of the few supply points and postal pickups in the cattle country, the Cribbs family was moving. Ella carelessly tossed the letter aside. For about a month, the unopened letter was forgotten, languishing in an old trunk. Once the family was settled, she rediscovered the letter, but her inclination was to disregard the whole affair. Only a great deal of pressure and teasing from her

---

27. Cribbs to Kieth, March 18, 1887.

sisters Maggie and Carrie persuaded her to answer this lonesome cowboy's query:

> *Dec. 12, 1886*
>
> *Unknown Miss. It is with pleasure I take the privlidge of writing to you asking you to corospond with me as I wish to corospond with you. Miss Ella a friend of yours recommended you to me.*
>
> *From an unknown,*
>
> *D.C. Kieth*[28]

Although tardy, a reply to his query was evidently forthcoming. Missing from the collection of letters, her first letter is likely the one that he said he carried until it became so worn that he burned it. His next letter, postmarked at Snyder on February 2, 1887, expressed his great pleasure in receiving her kind and welcome letter.

Earliest photo of D.C. Kieth Jr.

"I suppose," Kieth wrote, "That you would like to know what I follow and a bout what kind of man I am. I am twenty-five years of age, light complected and a small man. The work I follow is with cattle. I am only a poor lonely western cow boy. I know cow boys has a wild disperzision, but they is a grate many cow boys not half as wild as their names."

---

28. Kieth to Cribbs, December 12, 1886.

He went on to tell her what a pleasure it was to read a letter from a kind lady friend. Then he wrote, "They isent very many Ladies in this countrie though we manage to have a dance once in a while." Getting right to the point, Kieth asked, "Do you dance or air you a church member?"[29]

Ella later replied that she did not dance but she never missed attending one. She opined that she was going to be very lonely when her sisters went off to school. She alone would be left to help their mother with the housework and her father and brother Dan with the field work. "I [would] much rather work in the house than the field, though I have to do both," she confessed.

From Fort Spunky, Ella wrote that the continued drought was discouraging the farmers. Some had planted corn. Some had left their farms for railroad work, and some were not doing anything, just waiting for it to rain. She extended an invitation for Kieth to join them in their simple entertainment in celebrating the Fourth of July.

"You and your friend Mr. Jenkins must come down next summer & enjoy the protracted meetings and other gatherings with us, as that is the farmers holiday . . . We have Sunday school every Sunday morning & singing in the afternoon, & preaching three times a month. And we have a very interest[ing] spelling match evry Saturday night." Then apologizing for her inquisitiveness, she proceeded to ask, "Would it be too much to ask for your name in full?"[30] His answer, without comment, came in the next letter, with his signature: Daniel Crofford Kieth.[31]

He confided, "It hasn't rained in this part of the countrie for several months. Though I don't wonder at it not raining in cow

29. Kieth to Cribbs, January 29, 1887.

30. Cribbs to Kieth, March 20, 1887.

31. Daniel Crawford Kieth's own spelling of his middle name

countrie for they work Sunday as well as any other day." When not busy with cow hunts, some cowboys were forced into farm work on the few farms that raised mostly hay for the horses in winter. However, as early as 1885, Espuela Ranch manager S.W. Lomax began experiments with crops of alfalfa, sorghum, and kaffir-corn for ranch use. Even so, Kieth didn't think much would come of trying to make ranch country into a farming one. He cautioned her that she should not be offended if she failed to get prompt answers to her letters during the summer because he was "liable to be off on a cow hunt."[32]

Earliest photo of Ella Cribbs

Ella shared details with him from her life. After a good rain in mid-April, she helped her pa replant corn, and she planned a peanut patch in the sandy loam. With nine other ladies, she joined the Farmers Alliance, "the only secret society" to which she belonged. While the national organization promised to fight falling prices, exorbitant freight rates and other agrarian ills, the local Hood County branch encouraged farmers to pool resources, dispose of their cotton through a business agent, and assist other members with recommendations or employment.[33] She promised to send her photo and, in the meantime, awaited his by return mail, though she had to wait four more years to receive it. Modestly, she described

32. Kieth to Cribbs, March 27, 1887.

33. Farmer's Alliance Records, Minutes of Hood County, 187-1896, Microfilm H 776 Hood Co., Southwest Collection, Texas Tech University, Lubbock, Texas.

herself as very homely and rustic, and not very entertaining, while she imagined his life as a cowboy to be rough and lonely.

"Miss Ella, I am very much pleased with your photograph. Though I am sorrow that I haven't one of mine to send you though I will bee as good as my promis. I will send one the first chance," likely from his sister's home next winter—then he hedged, "if nothing happens more than I am expecting."

Kieth outlined the ranch routine. "Mr. Merriman and my self works in the branding outfit on the range. We have been working very hard for the last three weeks gatheran hirds for the trail. We have got two hirds ready to start now and when they leave we will half to go to gatheran another one. Then wen it gets off we will go to branding calves." He and Mr. Jenkins hoped to come down next summer, "though I gess it will bee most impossible."

Six weeks later, June 16, 1887, his ranch job changed from the branding outfit to cow hunting on the outside, searching the range outside his outfit's territory for big unbranded calves with mothers wearing the Spur brand. Often alone in the dangerous situation, the cowboy roped the calf, choked it down with a tight rope from his horse, and then flanked or threw it down to immobilize it. Then he made a fire, heated the brand and burned ownership on the calf before turning it loose to join the herd. To Ella he wrote, "I hope you will think of your friend in the West the Saturday before the forth of July. I am shure I will think of you, if I am living."

Another dangerous job entailed turning large herds from South Texas or smaller nester herds from entering the Espuela free range of 500,000 acres bounded on the south and west by barbed wire. Due to the threat of the highly contagious and fatal tick fever spread by the coastal longhorns, drovers intent on trespassing faced armed resistance and legal sanctions. Besides trampling the ranch's grass, the vast trailing outfits often picked up strays for their own herds or their beef provision, making their presence even more unwelcomed. One cattle baron fenced trail herds out of his own 100,000 acres in central Texas, but his trail driver threatened to breach the Spur Ranch perimeters by cutting wires and pushing cattle through for grass and water. Thereafter, provisions were made for a special fenced-in travel lane, supplied with water, but special agents were designated to prevent future trespassing.

In reference to her sister's friend, Kieth warned, "Tell Miss Maggie that Mr. J.C. is liable to get killed. The Espuela Company has him turning trail hurd round thaire pasture. Some of them [herds] air very hard to turn." Abruptly changing the subject, he quizzed, "Please, Miss Ella, alow me to ask you why you wanted to know my name in full."

In answer to Ella's question about how the people of his country felt about Prohibition, he wrote, "I haven't hird but very little about it though I am in hopes they will do away with Whiskey altogether." In fact, within the next year his ranch boss Lomax would notify Dockum's Store and his ranch employees that Prohibition was in effect for all Espuela Ranch employees. With that edict, the Espuela manager joined the JA's Charles Goodnight and the Matador Ranch's H.H. Campbell in refusing to hire any ranch employee discharged for drunkenness or stealing.[34]

Kieth had put in time with the Espuela Company from March 1886 to July 1887 and April to August 1888,[35] but the TO Ranch,

---

34. Holden, W.C. *The Spur Ranch* (Boston: Christophen Publishing, 1934), pp. 21-22.

35. Holden, W.C. *The Spur Ranch,* "List of Employees on Spur Ranch 1885-1909" (Boston, Massachusetts: Christophen Publishing, 1934), p. 215.

25 miles southeast, lured him away with better pay. His duty was riding around the beef pasture every day, until cow hunting commenced in the fall when he would ride all day, and then guard the cattle at night. Looking for sympathy, he asked Ella to imagine how tired a person could get working night and day for a month at a time. Although believing his labor was worth more in ranch country, Kieth dreamed of having a home of his own *if,* he added, he lived to be very old and had good luck.

A man who often asked very personal questions amid the small talk, Kieth asked, "Miss Ella, please allow me to ask your age as I don't think you told me how old you was. Youer photo looks to bee about 17." (She was 20 at the time of the photo.) From the batch camp, he described his routine: "They is three of us staying hear at this ranch now. One milks and one cooks and I wride the beaf pasture . . . We have lots of chickens and eggs at this ranch and we also have a patch of corn and irish potaos and a plum py evry once and a while. We are not the best cooks in the world, but we do the best we can." But, in closing, he returned explosively to the personal. "Miss, Ella why do you think of living an old maid. Do you prefear that kind of life. I had rather think a married life would bee a much happier life."

A few weeks later the drought at Fort Spunky was broken by a glorious rain, too late, however, to save the 20 acres of corn the Cribbs' family had planted. Some of their neighbors gathered their meager corn harvest in a meal sack.

Ella related of those distressing times, "Pa says he will try this country one more year, as he cant get away this year. We have been trying to go to Washington Territory for the last three years, but have failed. You ask why I spoke about being an old maid. I don't expect to be one if I can help it, for old maids like old bachelors' have to ware that name yet, as the poet says, 'They are all getting married but me.' My friends tell me I am to hard to please, but I don't think so. I would like to keep house for some nice young man, as keeping house is one of my greatest cares. I don't expect I could do my duty but would try as hard as any person."

"You ask how old I am. I was 20 years old when I had the picture taken I sent you. I was 22 years old the 27th of last Oct. I would like to have a complete disscription of your self if agreeable." Then she added the stinger, "I will look for your picture soon."

Apologetic about his "old maid" remark, D.C. allowed that they knew nothing about each other, only by reputations, but he was satisfied she was among the best girls in the world. Then he offered a proposal, "How do you think you would like to keep house in the west for a cowboy. I would like to have a nice young ladie to keep house for me. I wouldent bee able to live in a very fine house, though I would treat hir as well as I was able to."

Then he explained his actions at work. "I will tell you why I quit the Espuela outfit. They don't alow their men to buy cattle. I bought a bunch of cattle last spring and went to the Ranch and quit for I new if I dident quit they would turn me off this faul. Though this outfit [TO Ranch] had already told me they would give me $30 dolars per month and work the year round and let me hold my cattle with them."

The conundrum presented to Kieth was summed up by Elmer Kelton in his book, *The Day the Cowboys Quit.*[36] "In many cases ranches denied the cowboy the right to keep cattle of his own. It was argued that such an outside interest detracted from attention to the company's welfare. Some cowboys, moreover, were tempted to put their own brands on cattle that rightfully belonged to the company."

---

36. Kelton, Elmer. *The Day the Cowboys Quit* (Ft. Worth, Texas: Texas Christian Press, 1971), p. x (in Introduction).

From Jayton on November 9, 1887, Kieth started with a herd of beef cattle in an 85-mile push south to the Texas & Pacific Railroad shipping point at Colorado City. From the supply boom town, complete with saloons where fortunes were made or lost overnight, he wrote Ella that after the next 10-day cow hunt, he hoped to be through cow hunting for the year. In the meantime, he expressed sorrow that she must work so hard. He anticipated that day when she could live without doing hard work.

His own expectations, *if* he survived the hazards of the job, were to work on the range two or three years longer and then to marry. "I have made up my mind to mairrie when I am 30 years of age, if I should live to bee that old, provided I can . . . If I evr leave this country on a pleasure trip I am coming to see you, provided you air still single."

Her letter of February 17, 1888, brought a Valentine and a favorite poem from Ella, which read, in part:

> I dream of thee in dewy hours.
> I think of thee by day,
> I muse upon thy wining powers,
> When thou art far away.
> I love to live in love with thee,
> To walk thy pensive eye,
> To linger in thy memory,
> To soothe thy bosom's sighs.
> I fain would have thy love-lit face
> Forever turned on me.
> Oh, may we not in future trace
> One common destiny?

Finally, in answer to her question about his looks, D.C. replied with an accounting of himself. "Miss Ella, you wish me to give you a full description of my self . . . I will be 27 years old the 7th of next October., if I should live that long. My weight is this winter 150 lbs, my weight in the summer is generly 143. My hair is a little darker than yours. My eyes air gray. I am high temperd and I drink whiskey, though I can controle my self. I am stought and healthy & have ben all my life . . . I will look for a description of you self in next letter."

Perhaps inspired by her valentine, D.C. wrote, "I never did think I could love a pirson of whom I never saw, but you will please alow me to say that I love your letters & your name & your repuitation. Miss Ella, do you believe that you can think enough of me to promis me your hand & heart in Matrimonia. I only hope that you do. I am coming down in March if I can possible get off . . . I guess I will get off the train at Granberry to get to Ft. Spunky. If so how far is it from the rail road to whaire you live?" [37]

A partial letter with no date and no envelope was found in the tattered shoebox, wrapped around the tintypes of Ella and D.C. It seems to fit here because Ella wrote, "I would hate to answer your question in the affirmative now, & when you came we might disside aganst each other. If we should agree to marry how thankful we ought to be to Mr. Merriman for introducing us, even by letter . . . I will look for you this year. You must write me before you start so I will know when to look for you."

The Spur Ranch Records and a letter from Dockum's Ranch post office revealed that by May 1888, he was once again cow hunting for the Espuela. The payroll includes M. Merriman, T. [Tol] Merriman, and Kieth employed at the top cowboy rate of $30 a

---

37. Kieth to Cribbs, March 6, 1888. Kieth refers to Granbury in Hood County, Texas.

month.[38] Then with the seasonal slowdown due to the hot August days, Kieth was reassigned to outside work and tank building at the lower wage of $20 a month, as was the ranch's custom to adjust its rate of pay for the jobs at hand.

In September 1888, Kieth's name no longer appeared on the payroll of the Dickens County ranch. He had quit The Espuela Company and planned to quit running cattle for a living. In disagreement of his plan was his aunt and uncle, the Isom Linns who lived in King County, 50 miles east of Dockum's Store. They wouldn't agree to him leaving the country. So, as D.C. explained to Ella, "I will start to work to morrow for the Matador Company. They will pay me a little better wages."

Finding the cow camp at Tee Pee City to be especially lonely in the winter, the cowboy promised his aunt that he would buy a section of land with his uncle's help and settle down. Near the village of Benjamin in Knox County, D.C. planned on buying some state school land before the general work for the Matadors commenced in April. "I am trying now to get me a little home so I may be able to settle down some day & make my own living & be my own boss."

To Ella he apologized, "I am glad to know the ring suited so well . . . yes, I am really sorry I was so hasty in proposing." Clearing up any misunderstanding about his proposal, Kieth then scribbled with his pencil, "I am going to make you one more promise and I will fill it as sure as we both live until that time. I am coming to see you sometime between now and next spring." After writing from Dockum's Store very late at night where there was so much music and revelry he could hardly think, D.C. saddled his horse and rode

38. Spur Ranch, Payroll Records, Southwest Collection, Texas Tech University, Lubbock, Texas.

another three miles before he could unroll his tarp-covered bedroll and go to sleep.

The next day he tried to sum up his feeling once more when he wrote, "please alow me to say in plain words that you may know my intentions. I will treat you well and make you as good a living as I can. I am not a wealthy man by any means. I hope to always have plenty to eat and wear and plenty of good friends. I intend to have a little home and live at home before many more years. That is my intention, whether I will, I can't say for certin . . . Your true and faithful friend until death."

At the bottom of the second letter, D.C. signed his name and then added:

Goodby.

P. S. Direct your letter to the Matador Ranch, Motley County.

Back at the farm, she wrote to him on a gloomy, wet November day in 1888. "My time has been consumed in teaching and the detestable old cotton patch. I have lost [only] two days and a half in four weeks from picking cotton. Therefore, my hands have been too sore and tired to hold the pen . . . I have picked over 2,500 lbs of cotton this fall, 107 lbs. by noon one day. Pa says he intends to plant a big crop of cotton next year . . . I don't look to be as stout as I really am. All our family has been sick with the chill and fever, except sister Maggie and myself. It may be our time next for we have just got through eating and shivering over a fine watermelon, which pa cut and ma scolded all the time we were eating it."

Later she confirmed her feelings, "Rest assured that I will forgive you for being frank in expressing your thought & intentions.

Please excuse my simplicity . . . If we ever meet you would find me a rustic girl . . . " Nevertheless, she countered with the eloquent closing: "Deep in the well springs of memory, may a rich pearl of good wishes rest dedicated for your true and faraway friend."

By the end of November, Ella bragged that she had picked 6,000 lb. of cotton, 191 lb. her best day. However, the cost was a badly sprained right arm due to carrying and packing heavy cotton sacks. La Grippe was sweeping the country epidemic-like, but she looked forward to a Christmas tree and a lively time, if the Lord be willing. She expressed the desire that D.C. could be with her and the Cribbs family during Christmas. However, Ella interjected that after the holidays, she planned to go to school and could be tied up for about six months.

For whatever reason, Miss Ella's collection of letters retained only the envelope of his December 8, 1888, reply, postmarked Matador, Texas. In his longest letter yet, Kieth wrote on January 21, 1889, from Tee Pee City, where he spent the holiday alone. Despite prospects of trail driving herds to the Indian Nation [Indian Territory of Oklahoma], Colorado, or Montana in the spring and summer, he tried once again. "I will come down to see you in March if that is agreeable. Now I will not disseave you this time. Will shure come if nothing hapons more than I am expecting . . . if not I can prospond [postpone] coming until next faul." If she's agreeable to a March visit, he will come by train and drop a note from Fort Worth concerning his arrival. In the meantime, "I am happy to know I have the opportunity off answern you once more."

An absence of retained letters occurred until April when Ella wrote to the Matador Ranch and filled her missive with details of the social life of her community and companions. After May school was out, she opined that her daily companion would be labor in the field. She closed with "Many good wishes to you in your new home." His reply lamented about the lack of letters he'd received since February because of his work with the Matador Company at the Double Mountains, where he chose to cow hunt instead of trail work. He did not expect to be back in Matador to pick up letters until June or July, but he hoped that a long letter would be awaiting from his absent but kind friend.

In her next letter of October 4, 1889, Ella shared her ideas about marriage. "You spoke about marrying. I may be mistaken, but I think it is right to marrie when people can suit them selves & get their true companions. Though I have almost desided to be an old maid. If I live to see the 27th of next Oct. I will be 25 years old. Though I don't feel like I was out of my teens . . . If I ever marrie I want to get my equal in evry respect, & get a good husband & Make a good wife, & live & made happy in evry respect. Then our home would be heaven on earth."

By December the romance seemed to have cooled down, partly from the difficulty in his cow work of shipping the herds to market and burning fire guards around the plains pasture near Della Plain in Floyd County. Ella had posited the question of what they should do with the letters, photos, the hair chain she gifted to him (a keepsake created from her plaited hair, a common Victorian craft of the time), and the ring gifted to her, if they closed their correspondence or if either found a mate.

In a long account for a shy man, D.C. admitted, "Miss Ella I think a greadeal off you & also think you would make any man a good & tru wife. I only hope when I mairrie, if I ever, that I will get as good women for a wife as I think you would be. Well I will make you one more promis & will full fill it if it is in my power to do so. Provided it is agreeable with you. I gess I will stay out hear this winter & I will come to see you next spring. Though I want you to set the time for me to come. And I will sure come if nothing happens more than I am expecting. And if we donot suit each other we can still be good friends as ever. And if we do suit, my intentions will be to bring you back with me. Provided you will come. Please excuse me for talking so plain as we air straingers. Though you do not seam much like a strainger to me . . . if we suit each other I will have a home for you & will promis to treat you well & make you the best living I can."

Christmas 1889 came and went without letters until D.C. wrote on January 30, 1890, from Tee Pee City once again, expressing joy for a splendid day and dinner with neighbor Wells.[39] D.C. was boarding with Wells on the Tongue River[40] while feeding beef cattle to be shipped in April. Sad news was that his aunt, who was like a mother to him, died and was buried before he received word and was able to travel the 40 miles to the Isom Linn home.

After much parleying back and forth, Kieth finally made the long-awaited trip. He sent this note from the sheriff's office at Fort Spunky: "Miss Ella Cribbs, At Home. Compliments off D.C. Kieth to Miss Ella Cribbs—would like to call and see her today."

---

39. F.M. Wells is listed on the Matador Ranch Cowboy List with a start date of February 1888. Transcript located at Matador Land & Cattle Co. file at Motley County Museum, Matador, Texas.

40. Tongue River, also known as the South Pease River, flows through Motley County to Cottle County where it joins the Middle Pease River. The name refers to a legend that many buffalo (bison) died there of black tongue disease.

Later photo of Ella Cribbs

The answer was prompt. "Compliments of Mr. D.C. Kieth carefully received and accepted. You may call today about eleven o'clock, this Dec. the 25th 1890." The six-day stay undoubtedly went well. Later he scribbled a note aboard the train and mailed it in the mobile post office on Fort Worth & Denver Railway, writing, "I can certainly go to my work with a good & willing heart, for I can say my Xmas has ben the happiest Xmas to me for the past 10 years."

Over the next several months, Kieth continued to write from shipping points, near and far away. In Texas, letters came from railroad shipping points of Colorado City to the south and Childress and Giles to the north. Giles in Donley County was considered unlucky by the Matador hands because of fatal accidents, including drownings in a nearby deep lake, but it was the only watering place during drought years between the Canadian and Red Rivers.

D.C.'s letters to Ella were also postmarked from the northern markets of Fort Madison, Iowa; Chicago, Illinois; and De Graff, Kansas. De Graff, about 30 miles northeast of Wichita, Kansas was sometimes used as a grazing and fattening ground. Fort Madison was located in the southeastern tip of Iowa on the Mississippi River, relatively close to the major beef markets of St. Louis and Chicago.

When the Matador Land & Cattle Co. manager, H.H. Campbell, resigned in 1890, he began to represent the settler faction against the ranch's interest. On January 5, 1891, Campbell successfully submitted a petition to organize Motley County to the Crosby County Commissioners Court at Estacado. The court set up precincts and voting places for the population that enumerated 139 residents in 1890, whereby Campbell was elected Motley County judge. Intent on taking care of official business, D.C. Kieth accompanied his former employer and good friend, Judge Campbell, on a 60-plus mile wagon trip to Estacado, where D.C. posted a letter to Ella.

"I went to church today," he wrote on February 8, 1891, "for the first time since I left Hood Co.; it was a Quaker meeting. Most of the people out here in this town air Quakers and seame to be very nice and clever. This is the oldest town in northeast Texas. Our county was attached to this co."

Estacado had no dancing halls, saloons, or gambling halls, but did have churches, schools, a literary society, and a library. The Quaker community of about 240 people served as the judicial center for 10 counties. A trade center located in the center of vast ranching interests, Estacado shined with a courthouse, post office, newspaper, blacksmith shop, boot shop, two general stores, and a hotel that recorded 500 guests within 11 months. Refinements included a school, the South Plains Academy, and a sanitarium with two physicians who performed surgery, albeit under the trees.[41] With approximately 33 farms and over 1,200 acres under cultivation, the small group of Quakers was the first to farm and irrigate on the Southern Plains, raising a surplus of rice-corn,[42] oats, and barley for sale. They experimented with growing other crops, vegetables, and fruit, and in one case, planting forest trees on the treeless plains.

However, it was their plantings of cotton that drew bitter opposition from the ranchers in the area because cattlemen wanted to keep "squatters" out of cattle country. Besides the ranchers' opposition, many other factors contributed to decline to this promising settlement: a seven-year drought; a resurvey of land which left some without valid titles to their claims; limited economic and marriage opportunities for the young; a religious dispute over the use of a school building; and more importantly, the death of Parris Cox, the Quaker colony leader.[43] The death knell for Estacado, however, was the vote to change the county seat to Emma, thereby depriving the settlement of business from those on legal business for multiple counties.

Although living a lonely cowboy's life on the trail, D.C. went further to reveal to Ella his prospects for the future: some land and a place of his own in his home country. "Though we have a co. seat now & the name of it is Matador. I have 10 lots in town and my land is about 3 miles from town."

---

41. Jenkins, John Cooper. *Estacado, Cradle of Civilization and Culture on the Staked Plains of Texas* (Crosbyton, Texas: Quality Publishers, 1986), pp. 58, 73-75, 142.

42. Rice-corn was planted by the Quakers and by the Espuela Ranch as an experimental crop, with various sources describing it as a grain to be ground for flour or as forage for cattle.

43. Jenkins, John Cooper. *Estacado, Cradle of Civilization and Culture on the Staked Plains of Texas* (Crosbyton, Texas: Quality Publishers, 1986), p. 151.

On a section of school land which sold for $2 an acre with 30 years to pay, Kieth went in partnership with F.M. Wells, the man he had boarded with during the winter while living on one of the farms to supply the Matador Ranch. A well previously dug by the Matador Ranch proved to be within Kieth's claim, a fact noted by H.H. Campbell, who was then manager of the ranch, which brought his congratulations for such good luck. Indicative of the changing makeup of the cowboy culture, while boarding with the Moore family, Kieth went to an all-night dance of "Matador Farmers," which lasted from 4 p.m. to the following day at 9 a.m.

Friends in Motley County urged Kieth to run for the office of sheriff, but he figured if he continued to collect $20 a trip for shipping and the usual $30 a month for cow hunting, and to farm for the Matadors and work in the winter camp, he'd earn more than a sheriff could. His decision proved wise because the close race for sheriff caused a feud between two Matador cowboys vying for the office. Newly elected Sheriff Joe Beckham and rival Jeff Boone became involved in scuffle in the courthouse on February 17, 1892, with gunplay that eventually resulted in the death of Boone from lead blood poisoning.

Although acquitted in Boone's death, Sheriff Beckham was then accused of misappropriation of the county's tax money by using it for gambling. The newly court-appointed sheriff, George Cook, was bringing incriminating evidence to Beckham's trial in Seymour when Cook was gunned down by the deposed Sheriff Beckham. Beckham then mounted a black horse and took to the outlaw trail across the border into Indian Territory. Disagreements between the warring factions in the beleaguered county required Judge H.H. Campbell to call out the Texas Rangers to impose martial law and restore order. Lawmen pursued Beckham across the Red River border and killed him in a gunfight at an outlaws' hideout.[44]

In April 1891, the rains once again brought prospects for a good year for both rancher and farmer. Kieth hoped he would be among the successful farmers in the next year. "I have got post enough to fence a good feal [field], garden and yard . . . I have a good well on my land & good soft water." Hoping that her father would find a good piece of land, Kieth wrote, "Some ses this will be a good farming countrie & some ses it wont. So I don't know my self but I intend on trying it, though I don't expect to depend on farming altogether. So if I fail at one thing probly I will succeed at an other. They is sevral new farms opening up out hear this year."

In the meantime, although he promised to keep his word if she insisted, Kieth requested that "their time," set for July, be postponed until next winter, when he would be better fixed and at home most of the time. He went on to tell her about a recent tragedy. "They was a man killed at the ranch a few days ago, he left a wife & two little children, & I feel so sorrow for them, for they air very poor." Jeff Varner had been gunned down at the Matador wagon by J.B. McLeod over a disputed bad debt. Soon caught, McLeod and the corpse had to be guarded night and day by local citizens until a circuit riding judge appeared. The killing prompted a burial marked by a sandstone boulder and a move by citizens who did not relish guarding the prisoner night and day to petition for a jail house.[45]

---

44. Potts, Marisue. *Motley County Roundup: Over 100 Years of Gathering*, Second Edition (Matador, Texas: Mollie Burleson Ranch Ltd., 2020), pp. 92-97.

45. Potts, Marisue. "Hello Out There From the Jail," *Motley County Roundup: Over 100 Years of Gathering*, Second Edition (Matador, Texas: Mollie Burleson Ranch Ltd., 2020), pp. 103-105.

In June 1891, the hardest rains of several years created flash floods in the rising rivers and resulted in drowning of several people in the lower country. Although the rain and wind caused some damage to low-lying fields and water gaps, the moisture proved beneficial. "The man I am boarding with has a good crop of corn & wheat & oats. His corn feal [field] is clost to the river & the waters got all over the feal & disstroid a gradeal of the corn." Kieth, working with the beef outfit, wrote to Ella about seeing her brother Dan, who was working with the branding outfit and camped near the store at Tee Pee City. The "city" was a mere gathering of hovels and dugouts, originally a buffalo hunters' outpost on the Rath Trail, which included a general store and post office kept by Swedish immigrant Anna Benson Cooper.[46]

From De Graff, Kansas, D.C. next penned a note: "I shipped a train off cattle to this place which is to the pastured here until faul & then shiped to market. The blue stem grass is very fine in this country." He agreed to her date to marry, the 24th of December. "You air in my daily thoughts & seam nearer & dearer to me than any one on earth." Because he heard that her father was planning to come in search of a piece of land, he offered this bit of advice: "Sister [Sophronia Garner] ses your mother aught to come with your father if he comes in a wagon as it would be most shure to improve hir health."

While Ella was in a whirlwind of picnics, weddings, parties, protracted meetings, and literary society sessions, Kieth was off gathering wild mustangs. "I had ben running a bunach off wild horses all day & was very tired. So I coreld the horses after so long a time & brought them to camps today."

46. Potts, Marisue. "Anna's American Dream," *Motley County Roundup: Over 100 Years of Gathering*, Second Edition (Matador, Texas: Mollie Burleson Ranch Ltd., 2020), pp. 57-61.

Ranch work went on. "We have at this time 1700 head of beaf cattle under hurd & I think we will start for the rail road with them next Tuesday. & I expect I will half to go off with them, if I do I will be gone . . . a bout 12 or 14 days in all . . . Dan ses if his father dosent com this summer he will take up a section next winter & hold it until he [Philander Cribbs] can come."

Weighing the possibilities of the future, Kieth wrote, " . . . but as I am a poor man, I will just half to do the best I can . . . now you may get very lonely out here at times for this isent a settled countrie a tal to compare with that countrie, but [I] will never leave you a day longer by your self than I can help, now I want you to think all that over and be satisfied you air willing to come & help me climb the hill . . . if you should come out here with me & get dissatisfied I would be so sorrow, so I feal it my duty to explain what I have to you."

In August 1891, Kieth trailed a herd to the jinxed rail loading station of Giles. That particular shipping point on the Fort Worth & Denver Railway was about 50 or 60 miles from Tee Pee City. Because of the things that had happened there earlier, the cowboys preferred to load out at Childress, though it was farther away. "For very near evry hurd this out fit has drove to Giles, they has ben a man very badly hurt or killed. It seames to be an unlucky place," he wrote. James Carter, one of their men who had worked for the Matadors for five or six years, was badly injured when his horse fell with him. Carter never spoke again, and after almost two days, he died on the trail. Another hand drowned in the deep lake nearby.

Despite his fatigue or the crude conditions on the trail or shipping route, D.C. always tried to stay in touch. He scribbled, "My dear girl, I take my pencil in hand to neight to try & write you a few lines . . . Well, we air near the rail road to neight & think we will ship to marrow, that is if the cars comes so we can load our cattle. We have had very good luck coming up the trail so far . . . The Boys has all gone to bed except my self & 2 that is on first gard, & I am siting by my lantern trying to write to one who seames so dear to me. When I came in to supper this eavning & was unsadling my horse I thought off you & thought I would like to write you . . . as it might be sevral days before I can write . . . from Chicago."

By September 1891, Kieth wrote to Ella that her father seemed to be in love with the country. Cribbs agreed to live on Kieth's section during the coming year and make improvements for his future son-in-law. Cribbs indicated that he planned to move in the fall if he could get things together.

"I think youal will like this countrie, & think it will help your mothers health," D.C. reiterated to Ella. "I spoke to your Father a bout our marriage while he was out hear so he sed thair was no objections. You may think I was rather hasty but I thought it best as he was intending on moving out hear this faul if he could get ready before winter . . . I hope you will come with him this faul, for it will be better for us, for I will not be able to lose any more time than I can help, & we can get mairred out hear."

While her father was away, Ella and sister Carrie picked a bale and half of cotton. She answered her betrothed, "O we have so much to do to get ready to move by the time Pa wishes to start. I am indeed surprised to know Pa intends to make such a move as this with Ma & by private conveyance & that in winter. Ma was much anxious to take this trip last summer, but we concluded the weather was too warm & the journey too far for her then. I never saw any one more delighted with a country & its people than Pa is with your country. I am confident it would make Pa sick, if we should fail to get ready to move out there this year."

In October 1891 she wrote, "Pa hasn't been well since he came home—but is making calculations to start about the first of Nov. Ma says we can't leave her behind—she intends to start if she never gets there. She is in hopes the change will improve her health. Maggie has decided to go with us too, & give up the school she has engaged to teach in Hill County—for it is so sickly down there. My sisters children was exposed to the 'hooping cough, while here last summer, & she writes us they all have it, & the Dr. has given up the eldest as he has malriah, fever & pneumonia . . . They lost their youngest child the 14th of last July."

She reported that a fight between two local boys resulted in the fatal stabbing of one. "I wasn't at the partie, but attended the funeral, & it was the nicest corpse I ever saw . . . it seems like this neighbor-hood will never be free of trouble. I am glad Dan isn't here."

Worrying about their trip, Kieth wrote in late October, "I am afraid youal will have some bad weather coming out . . . please write to me a day or so before youal start . . . direct your letter to Matador . . . We call it two hundred miles from hear to Jacksboro, from thair on that way I don't know the countrie." He thanked her for his birthday present, a hair chain[47] of Ella's hair plaited by her sister Maggie.

Ella finished her cotton picking, weighing in at 6,800 lbs. "Carrie & I anticipate having a nice time & lots of fun on the road. I had my pony broke last summer & she says she intends to ride it

---

47. Hair work was a traditional Victorian craft using the beloved's hair as a personal senti-ment for showing affection or mourning by creating chains, jewelry, art objects, or pic-tures. Swedish folklore suggested that rings and bracelets of hair increased love.

out there . . . Yes you may come if you still wish to i.e. if we fail to get off. But Pa says he is bound to go this year."

Go he did, pointing the wagon, loaded with his family and as much of their personal items as possible, toward the Rolling Plains on November 4, 1891. Leaving Fort Spunky and the George's Creek[48] community, they skirted the Brazos River and headed in a northerly direction, averting Jacksboro. Making less than 20 miles a day, they stopped in Parker County at Whitt, a trade center of about 100 residents, to mail a card to Ella's brother Dan, asking him to come and meet them. A full day's drive ahead to Farmer, a village in Young County with a population of 125, Ella prepared a letter of woe to send to D.C. who was off on a cow hunt.

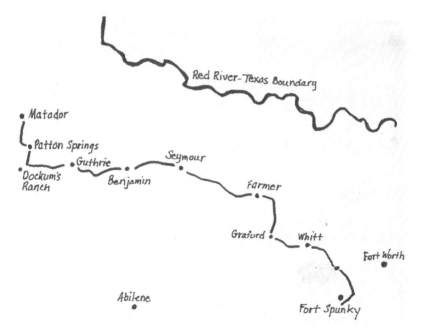

Map showing the route from Fort Spunky to the town of Matador

---

48. Maps show George's Creek, but Ella referred to the community just five miles away from Fort Spunky as "Georgia's Creek."

Jack Co. Tex.
Nov. 9th 1891
Mr. D.C. Kieth,
Matador, Tex.

Dear Friend:

If I can keep the sand & ashes out of my eyes long enough I will tell you where we are at & about our trip. We left last Wednesday the 4th of Nov. & this is the 6th day of our journey. As a real norther blew up last eve we are laying over in Jack Co. near the widow Estes place.

We traveled two days in the worst sand storms I ever saw—it is so dry we cn't hardly get drinking water much less stock water. As yet Mr. Turner hasn't over taken us yet, as he promised, but we are finding our way splendidly & we have had plenty company so far—only six wagons over taken us this side of Weatherford.

Pa mailed Dan a card at Whitt, yesterday morning asking him to meet us (i.e., if he can get off) as we are heavy loaded—as yet we haven't traveled more than 18 miles in a day. If we ever do get to Matador I hope we never make another long move like this. I am afraid that Pa & Ma can't stand much exposure. It is over a days drive to Farmer. Will not go via Jacksboro, but will go via Seymour.

I had you two letters mailed last Tues. to Teepee City, doubtless they have been forwarded to you by this time. I recd. a letter from you last Sat. & was glad you appreciated your chain. Maggie made it for me last spring while she was taking lessons in hair work. She has since given me lessons in the same accomplishment.

Oh! How I do wish we were at our destination. The wind is blowing hard & cold. I will mail this to you at the first P. O. but don't know where that will be.

Pa has just come in from hunting water & he informs us we about one mile from the widow Kieth's. I suppose she is a relation of yours. We are now on the Graham road & Mr. Jno. B. Estes is at home and fraiting on another road about 7 miles from this one. We are camped in a flat at the foot of a hill, where there is fine post oak timeber. I hope to see you and Dan soon.

As ever   Ella

Choosing not to take the stagecoach route from Weatherford to Jacksboro and beyond, the wagon headed toward a less traveled road to Seymour in Knox County. A long pull remained over the ascending plateaus, including the divide between the Wichita and Brazos watershed ridge called "the Narrows," located in Knox County. On the north side, the Wichita River drained to the Red River and the Mississippi, but on the south side the Brazos River drained into the Gulf of Mexico.

Yet to come was "the Wichita Hades," in the Wichita River breaks of King County before hitting Dockum's Ranch store in the rolling plains of Dickens County. From there the lower plains took them north to Patton Springs, named for a buffalo hunter of the 1870s. Crossing the Tongue River at Sanders' Hollow, also named for the camp of two buffalo hunters, the wagon hit the Tee Pee Flat Road, once part of the Old Rath Trail that supplied buffalo hunters and freighters. Fifteen days after their shaky departure from Fort Spunky, the Cribbs wagon pulled into the Matador Ranch's MacDonald Camp, where D. or "Dee" MacDonald and his wife, Dora, known by the cowboys affectionately as "Mammie Mac" or "Mittie," served the ranch's interests as camp man and laundress/cook.

When the struggling Cribbs' entourage finally arrived on November 19, 1891, Kieth was not there to greet them. He was boarding at one of the company farms about six miles from Tee Pee City, where he was fencing. Four days after their arrival, he wrote tersely to his betrothed, the one who had just made the trip from hell to become his bride in a few weeks.

"I wish I could come up at once, though I have about 4 days work to do down hear & cant come at present with out letting my work go undon. So I will come next Friday or Saturday if possible, so good eavning."

The next day after rolling into the Matador area and bedding down at MacDonald Camp, Mrs. MacDonald insisted that the weary family attend a ball in Matador, a few miles north of the camp, to get acquainted. Soon the blacksmith's wife, Mrs. Frank Baxter, was engaged to make a wedding dress for the petite Ella. The dressmaker, formerly from Kansas City, claimed the only sewing machine in the county. Mrs. Baxter designed a two-pieced basque style with a close-fitting bodice, consisting of gray cashmere and velvet, set off with 24 steel buttons.[49]

A few short weeks later on December 23, 1891, the *Motley County News* announced the second wedding recorded in the newly organized county, but the first one that physically took place there. "On this morning at 9 o'clock A. M. at the residence of Mrs. Mittie McDonald's, Mr. D.C. Kieth wed to Miss Ella E. Cribbs, Esq.

---

49. Keith (Kieth) Family Collection, Motley County Museum, Matador, Texas, includes letters, a wedding dress, a framed marriage certificate, a photograph of the bride and groom, and a newspaper clipping describing the wedding.

McHugh officiating. Mr. Kieth is one of Motley County's most in-
dustrious young men, while Miss Ella, who has been amongst us but
a short time has gained the love and affection of all. Mr. Walter A.
Walton and Mr. H.L. White, acting as groomsmen, and the bride's
two lovely sisters, Miss Maggie and Miss Carrie, acting as bridesmaids.
May their pathway be strewn with flowers and no sorrow ever be their
lot in the best wishes of a friend." (No doubt, Miss Carrie Cribbs, one
of the few young ladies available, was quickly snapped up to become
the bride of Mr. Walter Walton, the first County Clerk.)

Wedding photo of Daniel Crawford Kieth and
Ella E. Cribbs on December 23, 1891

The pathway was to be strewn with the startling hues of wild-flowers: the fuchsia, yellow, and green blossoms of cactus, the flaming reds of the firewheel (gaillardia or Indian blanket), the brilliant spires of purple gayfeather (Liatris) or the muted orchid of forever summer (purple aster). Many rainy seasons and droughts to come provided the golden tones of buffalo and grama grasses and the surprising russets of blue stem varieties.

The following January of 1892 was a bitter winter, and the spring and summer brought no rain for the parched, overstocked range. Cattle and horses gnawed on the knee-high brush of shinnery oak as the unceasing wind blew away the tilled earth, leaving only the shiny mark of the plow on the sod. Many people starved out and once again moved on to the next prospect of cheap land and a brighter future.

The Kieths, however, persevered. Their first humble home, a half-dugout at the Matador Ranch's line camp on Turtlehole Creek, was soon replaced by a similar setup on Rustler Creek. The feeder branch of the South Pease River earned that ominous name in 1879 when Frank Collinson joined a New Mexico crew of Coggin & Wiley's outfit in trailing cattle to Blanco Canyon and the Rolling Plains.

The men proceeded to construct corrals, new dugouts, and better headquarters at the edge of the Caprock when some suspicious characters showed up. R.K. Wiley's thinly disguised nephew was warned, "Don't rob this outfit unless you expect a considerable scrap." The would-be thieves left, but their camp was found along the waterway that was thereafter known as Rustler Creek.[50]

---

50. Collinson, Frank. *Life in the Saddle* (Norman: University of Oklahoma Press, 1963), p. 119.

D.C. And Ella Kieth and three children

The Matador Ranch dugout was built back into a hill, straddling the boundary line of Motley and Dickens counties. A later occupant said that she lived in Motley but milked the cows in Dickens. In the beginning, the walls were covered with cheesecloth to stabilize the dirt walls and deter the entry of creepy crawlies, scorpions, and centipedes. What evolved into a three-room abode with a porch was warm and cozy. A hole dug in the shade of a tree or the cool waters of the creek sufficed as a refrigerator of sorts. While D.C. longed for that home of his own, the one he often wrote about, and a time he could work for himself, for the next 11 years the Kieths lived at Rustler's Line Camp. Long after the family moved onto their own homestead next to Grandpa Cribbs, Kieth continued to ship cattle for the Matadors. Ella, who despised the thought of being an old maid at 26, got busy and had a "paccel" of kids. The 1900 Census taker noted Sue, age 7, Mary, age 6, Gilbert, age 4, Danial P. [Daniel or D.P.], age 2, and Sophie H. [Hester], age 1. The sixth child, Charlie, would be along "dreckley" [directly] in 1905. Sometime after the family moved to Motley County, they started using the Keith spelling of their name.[51]

The Mott Camp log cabin and new line camp house, circa 1910, with Grandpa P.A. Cribbs, Mary Keith, and Sue Keith Alley's child, Sue Carrie Alley

Sue Keith, the oldest child, left the nest by the next census when she turned 17. She married a clean-cut cowboy, Bob Alley, who took her to live at the Cottonwood Mott Line Camp in 1911. When her sister Mary came to visit, the girls often rode a few miles to

---

51. Hereafter, the family used the Keith family spelling of the their name, instead of Kieth.

Lyman Post Office to pick up their mail. Kodaking, being a popular pastime of the era, recorded the family's efforts with photographic images of the infamous log cabin where two men killed each other over the singing of the song "Yankee Doodle Dandy."

A photo of Sue Keith Alley on horseback in front of the recently built frame house attests to her beauty and grace, while giving an estimation of when the white frame, four-room house was built. Sue may have had an above-ground home before her mother, Ella, did.

Photo of Sue Keith Alley on horseback at the Mott line camp

D.C. and Ella's son Gilbert Keith went to work for the Matador outfit, working cattle and cooking at the chuckwagon. Whenever the wagon was close to the headquarters or a nearby camp, the ladies dressed up in their finest attire and fancy hats to ride out for a visit. The cook was always eager to exchange the women's homemade pies and cakes for some freshly killed beef, which without refrigeration wouldn't last long anyway.

When Sue suffered an attack of appendicitis, she and Mary were rushed by Pierce Arrow touring car over bumpy dirt roads to catch the train at Quanah for Fort Worth. From St. Joseph's Infirmary, Mary wrote a postcard to Sue's husband Bob Alley at Lyman Post Office, saying that the doctor would operate on April 30, 1912. Tragically, just two and a half years later the young mother had a relapse, and the second operation took place under lantern light in the kitchen of the Keith family home. The doctor was unsuccessful in saving her life. She passed away on December 29, 1914. Her marble gravestone in East Mound Cemetery has a ceramic photo of the young woman, dressed in finery, standing with her horse. The inscription reads simply: A Cowboy's Daughter, A Cowboy's Wife. This beautiful flower of a daughter was plucked far too young.

In 1907, 16 years after their marriage, D.C. and Ella left the somewhat improved half-dugout at Rustler Camp and finally moved south of Matador to the home he promised her so long ago.

D.C., a loyal and treasured employee of the Matador Ranch, had been in charge of shipping cattle for 40 years. He passed away in 1933, at age 72. In 1940, Mary and her widowed mother, Ella, moved into Matador to a new house that was adorned with native rock. With her wry sense of humor, Ella, who had lived in a dugout or half-dugout from 1891 to 1907, commented

Daniel Crawford (D.C.) Kieth (Keith)   that she had waited 50 years for that house.[52] She passed away in 1943 at age 79 and joined D.C. and Sue in the family plot at East Mound Cemetery, Matador, Texas.

Miss Mary, with her collection of photographs and stories about the early cowboys, and her youngest brother Charlie, with the family treasures he shared with the Motley County Museum, became the historians of the family. Charlie and Viola Keith's cattleman son, Dave, also had a wonderful recollection of the family and county history that he so generously shared. A graduate of West Texas State University with a B.S. degree in agriculture, Dave worked for the Natural Resources Conservation Service and ran cattle in New Mexico, in Motley County on the Cribbs/Keith section, and in Dickens County. His brother Charles Robert Keith graduated from Texas A&M, served in the Vietnam Conflict, and earned the rank of major in the U.S. Marine Corps. When Charles Robert retired in Matador, he embarked on community development and spread word in the rural community of a new innovation, the World Wide Web Information Highway. After a successful stretch of community development, Charles Robert retired to Georgetown, Texas.

In the shadow of the Caprock, on the Rolling Plains, the cowboy D.C. Kieth (Keith) became both a cotton farmer and a stock raiser. He and his wife, Ella Eugenia Cribbs Kieth (Keith), symbolized the melding of the Southern cotton culture and the Cross Timbers ranching tradition in Motley County, where the economy became supported by livestock *and* agriculture, including not only wheat, hay, and sorghum milo but also King Cotton.

According to their youngest son, Charlie, if his mother Ella ever had to pick another boll of cotton, he wasn't aware of it.[53]

---

52. Traweek, Eleanor. *Of Such as These: A History of Motley County* (Quanah, Texas: Nortex Publishers, 1973), p. 284.

53. Keith, Charlie. Personal interview to Marisue Potts, October 1996, Motley County Museum, Matador, Texas.

D.C. and Ella Kieth (Keith) with six of their children plus their horses and mules; the children (from left) are D.P., Charlie, Sue, Mary, Helen, and Gilbert

The Long March: The Story of Philander Cribbs

The name Philander Cribbs kept surfacing in the letters written between D.C. Kieth (Keith) and Ella E. Cribbs. Ella's father was looking for a better climate to benefit his and his wife's health. He seemed frail and sickly at age 55, and less than commendable by depending upon his daughters to pick cotton, help on the farm, and keep house for his delicate wife. Cribbs remained a mysterious character who, nevertheless, figured in the settlement of the newly organized Motley County by bringing the cotton culture to ranch country.

While researching information about Civil War Veterans buried in East Mound Cemetery for the files of the Motley County Museum, this researcher tapped the Texas State Archives for pension information. The documents provided War Department records, applications of veterans and widows, letters, and petitions with valuable information of special interest to the historical museum and helped to preserve the history of the people, the county, and the region.

This collected information revealed that Philander A. Cribbs petitioned the state of Texas in 1926 for a reinstatement of a pension, based on his need and service to the Confederate States of America during the Civil War.[54] The state government, which allowed only $300 income a year for its pensioners, had determined that 90-year-old Cribbs had too many assets to continue to receive a pension.

In his own handwriting, Cribbs laid out his plea to reinstate his pension. "I drew it regular for about two years. It was discontinued on account of my holding a section of School Land which I had filed on and paid all charges and lived according to the Law, requiring three years of occupation. I had to borrow the money to make these payments, also filing and necessary expences. I had no money. Nothing but a wagon, a span of horses, wife and five children.

"Consequently," he wrote, "I found it a hard matter to make a living in a new country, but we wanted a 'Home' and this was my chance tho a hard one to get it. So I aplide for a Pension—got it and soon lost it on account of owning—and paying Taxes on this section of land. I disposed of the land in the following manner—I deaded 160 acres to my oldest Daughter. I also deaded 320 acres to my 2nd Daughter with the understanding that my wife and I should have this as our home as long we lived.

"We had only one Son who was mining in Arizona, working in Cooper Quean Mines and had contracted the Copper Flue-Consumption."

The Copper Queen Mine, one of the largest underground copper reserves, had the reputation of using their miners hard and forcing them to work under adverse and dangerous conditions. The workers' safety was often disregarded, and sometimes the mine did blasting while workers were in the tunnel. Lighting was dim, requiring Dan Cribbs to use his metal candle holder, stuck in the mine

54. P.A. Cribbs Records, Texas State Archives, State of Texas, Dec. 10, 1926. Letters from Comptroller's Dept., State of Texas, Dec. 10, 1926, and Adjutant General, War Department, Washington, D.C., Dec. 11, 1926.

wall, to light his pickax efforts. The grim reminder of hard times is displayed at the Motley County Museum with his photograph from World War I.

Philander went on to say that to get his ailing son to live with them, he and his wife Nannie deeded Dan'l Cribbs the remaining 172.6 acres of their section. Just two years after his mother's death, Dan'l died on March 11, 1918, at age 48. Thereafter, Cribbs' income consisted of the meager rentals off the small acreage as provided in the trust established for their son.

"I have no other Income. I am past ninety years old. I get about pretty well and love to go to the United Confederate Veterans (U.C.V.) annual re-unions and see the Dear Old Boys in Gray and have a good time with them. It makes me feel young again."

Cribbs was active in the efforts of Camp Maxey, No. 860 Chapter of the UCV, and used his influence to see that the graves of those local men who had passed away were marked with an Iron Southern Cross of the Confederate States of America. One of those so honored was Ridgley Greathouse, who died in obscurity on the Matador Ranch but had been involved in the Chapman Affair of 1862, a failed conspiracy to pirate Union gold to benefit the Confederacy.[55]

P.A. Cribbs, Infantryman in a "Modern" War

In his plea for his pension, Cribbs provided us with a foot soldier's story, as he recalled it 65 years later. Although admittedly shy on dates, Cribbs presented a written account of his army record in a matter-of-fact manner. He dwelt neither on the hardships of being in

---

55. Potts, Marisue Burleson. *Ridgley Greathouse: Confederate, Conspirator, Convict, and Capitalist* (Matador, Texas: Mollie Burleson Ranch Ltd., 2021).

the infantry on the losing side nor the bitter taste of defeat involving "hard" war,[56] surrender, occupation, and punitive reconstruction.

Although traditional warfare, as practiced in the Napoleonic wars, involved armament by muzzleloaders, transport by animal power, cavalry fighting, frontal assaults, decisive one-day battles, and defensive maneuvers—such as the "hollow square" in which several lines of armed soldiers face outward on four sides, ready to repel an enemy or cavalry from any direction. Cribbs, although perhaps unaware of it as events unfolded in 1861, became immersed in a new and more deadly type of war, a "modern" war made possible by technological innovations and evolving military strategies.

Using the criteria established by historian James McPherson,[57] in this type of modern war Cribbs could come face-to-face with conscription; new types of armament such as rifles, rifled artillery, and repeating rifles; trenches for protection against the more powerful firepower; naval use of ironclads and submarines; mass production to manufacture military goods; utilization of railroads and telegraphs; and airborne observation. In this new warfare, generals who had studied the Napoleonic wars were forced to develop new strategies to deal with the uniqueness of a vast and geographically diverse American theatre.

Pre-War Alabama Roots

Born in 1836 in Tuscaloosa, Alabama, Philander Alexander Cribbs was the third of nine children. His father, Daniel Cribbs, a salt-glaze

---

56. The term "hard war" was used opposed to "total war," in this context because women and children were not pursued or killed as they were in the war waged by the U.S. Army against Native Americans in the 1800s.

57. McPherson, James M. *Ordeal by Fire: The Civil War and Reconstruction* (New York: McGraw Hill, 1992), p. 183.

potter and stoneware manufacturer, had moved from Ohio in 1827. The elder Cribbs prospered so well that 10 years later he was taxed $8.32 on 440 acres, 10 slaves, a pleasure carriage, a silver watch, a metal clock, and $450 in currency. While serving as the local sheriff in 1842, Daniel invested in the steamboat *Tuscaloosa* to carry goods, including his pottery, down the Black Warrior River to the port of Mobile, Alabama. When the steamboat exploded in 1845, his business suffered so much that he relocated the family to California, capitalizing on the Gold Rush.

Crossing through the Isthmus of Panama, the family returned to Tuscaloosa in 1850. Daniel invested his new windfall in slaves to help operate his jug factory and grist mill. Despite his ownership of slaves, the entrepreneur apparently still had emotional ties to the North. On the Census of 1860, which employed both Daniel and his son Philander as census enumerators, Daniel signed the last page with his signature and the words "Faithful Ohio."[58]

Philander, evidenced by the letters received by his sweetheart Nannie McShann, was a man of some education who sometimes wrote poetry. As the daughter of slave owners, she was a pampered young woman whose every need was catered to by a slave who even slept in her room.[59] She also spent her time writing poetry, going to social gatherings, and attending protracted religious meetings. The romance between Philander and Nannie resulted in their marriage on November 28, 1860, at Eutaw in Green County, Alabama,[60] just six weeks before Alabama voted 61-39 in favor of secession.

---

58. Cribbs Collection, Motley County Museum, Matador, Texas.

59. Traweek, Eleanor. *Of Such as These: A History of Motley County* (Quanah, Texas: Eakin Publishers, 1976), p. 223.

60. Cribbs, Bill. "A Brief Biography on Daniel C. Cribbs," *Cribbs (Krebs) Family Newsletter*, Volume 1, Edition 1 (Channelview, Texas: Bill Cribbs, Nov. 1991), p. 1.

In September 1861, while Union forces occupied northern Kentucky and threatened an invasion of Tennessee, pro-Union supporters burned bridges and attacked Confederate supply lines in anticipation. Philander Alexander Cribbs enlisted for 12 months as a Confederate volunteer. He mustered in at Opalaca as a 3rd lieutenant in Company K of the 20th Alabama Infantry Regiment.[61] They marched 150 miles south to drill at Mobile, where they were quartered in the Old Dog River Factory building.

On December 2, 1861, with General J.M. Withers commanding, regiment records reveal that 836 were present and accounted for. By February, the Army of Mobile, which had been included under General Braxton Bragg's department of Alabama and Florida, was ordered to Tennessee. When the Confederate Congress passed the conscription law in April 1862, which made current enlistees and those 18-35 years old liable for three years' service, the Army of Mobile was marching to Knoxville for active service under Major General Edmund Kirby Smith.

Whether dimmed by memory, misinformation, or enhanced by wartime braggadocio, Cribbs offered an implausible accounting of the following event:

We marched all night through a drizzly rain over the mountain and attacked General Seigle's [referring to Major General Franz Sigel] division of Germans, fresh from Germany at London, Kentucky, also at Barber's Town [Barbourville]. They were at breakfast and altogether surprised. Consequently, not much of a fight, tho we killed many of them and took about

---

61. Cribbs Collection, Motley County Museum, Matador, Texas. P.A. Cribbs file, including war record, application, letter of disqualification, reapplication, and handwritten account from Texas State Archives, Austin.

15,000 prisoners, also a great quantity of ammunition and stores. We armed ourselves with new Enfield rifles; our arms were old British "Flint and Steele" muskets, converted to percussion cap locks.

Cribbs estimation of the number of prisoners taken doesn't stand up to the volumes of Civil War data collected in the intervening years. As an infantryman in a brigade, the rumors received in the ranks were not likely the most reliable. Some valuable information, however, can be gleaned from his account.

No doubt the importance of capturing arms, ammunition, and stores from the Union to be used by the Confederates cannot be exaggerated. The Confederates' effective firing range would be increased from about 80 yards for the musket to 400 yards for the Enfield, allowing a greater edge against frontal assaults or cavalry attacks.[62] Ammunition, always in short supply, would be a windfall.

Franz Sigel, appointed by President Lincoln, received credit for successfully raising 200,000 American-born Germans and 250,000 first-generation Germans for the Union army, creating the largest ethnic contingent among many foreign-born volunteers, mercenaries, and former revolutionaries in their own country.

In reliable accounts, the Wildcat Mountain Battle near New London, Kentucky, involved 6,000 Confederates under Swiss-born Brigadier General Felix Zollicoffer, who was sent to protect the Cumberland Gap from a small Union presence. Zollicoffer seized a camp near Barbourville and collected salt, equipment, and arms, likely the source of Cribb's Enfield rifle acquisition. Reinforcements for the Union under Polish-born Brigadier General Albin F. Schoepf

---

62. McPherson, James M. *Ordeal by Fire: The Civil War and Reconstruction* (New York: McGraw Hill, 1992), p. 197.

led to a Confederate retreat.[63] Perhaps Schoepf was the name Cribbs recalled as "Seigle."

Some 10,000 of Edmund Kirby Smith's 18,000 invading Confederate troops marched through drought-stricken Kentucky, pulling wagonloads of weapons available to arm any Kentuckians who joined their cause. Though takers from Southern sympathizers were few, the Confederates made an attempt to establish a secessionist government at Frankfort, Kentucky. Cribbs recalled, "History says that Kentucky never had a Confederate governor, but I was in line of a Hollow Square and witnessed the inauguration of Haws."

An account in Confederate Military History[64] supports his eye-witness account, noting "Upon the death of Gov. George W. Johnson, who fell on the second day at Shiloh while fighting in the ranks, the legislative council [of the Confederate Congress] elected Honorable Richard Hawes as his successor. While the State [Kentucky] was occupied by the Confederate army under General Bragg, Governor Hawes was inaugurated with due formality, and he delivered an inaugural address in the capitol at Frankfort, Oct. 4, 1862, but the evacuation of the place the same afternoon prevented his performance of any of the functions of a governor except the occupation of the executive mansion for a few hours."

Threatened by the approach of two of General Don Carlos Buell's Union divisions, Smith's troops were diverted from their moment of history. Cribbs said they received orders to "double-quick" march to reinforce General Bragg at Perryville where he was engaged with Buell's troops. On the way, their march was halted,

---

63. The Battle of Wildcat Mountain; www.battlefields.org.

64. Evans, Gen. Clement A., ed. *Confederate Military History: A Library of Confederate States History*, Vol. IX (New York: The Blue Grey Press, 1962), p. 215.

and they were ordered to cook three days' rations. The missed Battle of Perryville had been a standoff, but General Bragg was quitting Kentucky, and so was Edmund Kirby Smith's infantry with Cribbs' Alabama unit. Slowed by the sick and wounded and, short of supplies, the retreating forces fortunately were not pursued by Buell. Cribbs' 20th Alabama Infantry went into winter headquarters at McMinnville, Tennessee. There, during a bitter winter, his brigade reorganized, and the men reenlisted for an additional three years or the duration of the war—a daunting prospect.

Alabama Troops to Vicksburg

In the late spring, all Alabama troops were placed under General E.W. Tracy and ordered to march to Mississippi, where Cribbs' infantry was "taking position on Chickasaw Bayo in time to see the Yanks retreating to their gunboats above Vicksburg. From there," he wrote, "we were ordered to Port Gibson below Vicksburg. This was about the 1st of May 1863." Their goal was to counteract General U.S. Grant's plans to subdue Vicksburg and thereby control the Mississippi River. After five attempts to either bypass the river port by digging canals or flanking the city by navigating troops through the maze of waterways, Grant's new plan called for a joint navy-army operation. He proposed running the Union gunboats and supply boats past the Confederate batteries while the infantry, cut off from a base or a supply line, would march double-quick down the west bank to rendezvous with the fleet below Vicksburg.

Cribbs recalled, "We met General Grant's army—engaged them all day to late in the afternoon. They charged the entire line with a great force and drove us back with loss. Genl. Tracy was killed and Col. I.W. Garrett [Garrott] was promoted to Brigadere General and took comand of the Brigade. The second day after that we met Genl. Grant's Army in battle at Bakers Creek where we were again defeated and retreated to the Brest-Works around Vicksburg where we were besieged daily without interruption for 52 days."

Eyewitness to the 52-day siege of Vicksburg, Mrs. James M. Loughborough[65] had fled the Union's destruction of the railroad town of Jackson to be near her soldier-husband in Vicksburg. From a cave in the bluff and later a soil-covered bunker, she watched the tired and discouraged Confederates stream into the 4,500 population of a bluff town already suffering from a shortage of food and supplies. She observed the Federal encampment, the wagon trains bringing in supplies for the Union forces, and the gunboat activity on the Mississippi. She and other lady spectators viewed from the courthouse cupola the shelling from a Union bombardment. During a later assault, however, she also experienced the terror of screaming and exploding bombs that sent electrical shocks through her body. Incendiary bombs fell on the hillside town, catacombed with so many protective caves and trenches to earn it the name of "prairie dog village."[66]

General U.S. Grant, who impatiently wished to send his soldiers off to other theatres of war, did not want to wait for the age-old strategy of siege warfare to work. Since he had seen demoralized Rebels run in other battles, he expected their resistance to quickly crumble. Therefore, he launched a frontal assault on the fortress, which presented a bottleneck for passage on the Mississippi River. As the 13th U.S. Infantry charged the hillside, the Rebs above

65. Loughborough, Mrs. Jas. M. *My Cave Life in Vicksburg* (Spartanburg: Reprint Co., 1976), p. 100.
66. Miers, Earl Schenck. *The Web of Victory: Grant at Vicksburg* (New York: Alfred A. Knopf, 1955), p. 231.

lobbed shells with fuses cut short, creating disastrous effects on the Yanks. When the second assault also failed, Grant set his engineers to planning trenches and mines to blow up gaps in the Confederate line. So that his troops could continue digging, they devised "sap-rollers," a moving protective cover composed of two kegs filled with dirt and lashed together by willow saplings. Thus, two men could dig with less fear of rifle fire or Minnie balls raining down on them.

The Union's firepower included 220 gun types, among them Parrott rifles, Dahlgrens, Howitzers, smooth bores, Napoleons, siege guns, and field pieces.[67] In addition, artillery fire from the ironclads on the river or batteries across the river resulted in a bombardment that caused soldiers, as well as civilians, to suffer almost constant headaches and an increase in their psychological stress.

As the siege continued, other complaints surfaced: (1) bilious diarrhea caused by poor sanitation and drinking contaminated or mud-puddle water, (2) the poor quality of food, such as the coarse pea meal which prompted some to prefer to eat rats, and later when available, mule meat, (3) scurvy from a steady diet of salt pork without any green vegetables, (4) extreme irritation and discomfort from chiggers and mosquitoes, (5) chills and fevers of malaria, and (6) boredom, which was surprising under the circumstances. The men from opposing forces, entrenched so close together, relieved their boredom as they cross-talked, gossiped, joked, and traded news with or about folks or relatives from home.

Concerning the siege, Cribbs offered another bit of "unwritten history" from his memories. He wrote, "The 42nd Alabama Infantry Regiment occupied a fortress which was quite annoying to the enemy on the opposite side of the lines—so much that General

---

67. Ibid., p. 226.

Grant had a tunnel dug under it and mined it with a heavy charge, blowing it up, killing and wounding 2/3 or more of our men, and perfectly demoralizing those that was left." After the explosion the redoubt filled with charging Yanks.

General S.D. Lee then sent Colonel E.W. Pettus to the rear to secure reinforcements from Colonel T.H. Waul's Texas Legion. Pettus called for 60 volunteers to fall in line to retake the fort, and capture and kill the Yanks. Waul objected to letting Pettus have the men from his outfit and insisted on taking them in himself, but Pettus firmly pointed to his written orders. Waul, seeing he was defeated, laid down his uniform coat and sword. Then he buckled on a cartridge belt and shouldered a gun, taking his place in the ranks as a volunteer and made the charge with his men. Pettus ordered the men to fix bayonets in their guns without bullets, follow in single file, keep low, and wait for him to wave a red handkerchief before giving the Rebel yell as they charged.

Waul's report of the assault of May 2, which failed to mention his participation, related that "they retook the fort, drove the enemy through the breach they entered, tore down the stand of colors still floating over the parapet, and sent it to the colonel commanding the Legion, who immediately transmitted it with a note to General (S.D.) Lee."[68] According to Cribbs, there were two brigadier generals made that day. T.N. Waul and E.W. Pettus were promoted, and Pettus was later destined to lead the Alabama brigade, including Cribbs, on Lookout Mountain.

Cribbs had no mention in his summary of the hardships during the siege, but others recalled that the food shortage in Vicksburg

68. Evans, General Clement A., editor. *Confederate Military History*, Vol. VI (New York: Blue & Grey Press, Thomas Yoseloff, 1962), p. 121.

may have led to a scarcity of rats, dogs, and mules. At one particularly low point, Mrs. Loughborough resorted to having a servant boil a pet bird so that her daughter might have the nourishing broth. In recounting her experiences, she mentioned events that were seen and experienced by defenders: a truce to bury the putrifying bodies on the hillsides; the ironclad *Cincinatti* being struck; the hail of iron from the bombardment, making furrows in the hillside; the misery of rifle pits saturated with rain; the awful sanitary conditions with men drinking from mud puddles; soldiers fighting in hand-to-hand combat and using hand grenades; the 4 a.m. shelling that propelled maiming shrapnel; the artillery targeting of civilians, churches, and hospitals; and the white flag of surrender flying over the fort.

One particular event seemed to rankle Cribbs the most, even after 65 years. Although his army surrendered on July 3, "General Grant refused to accept the surrender until the next day, that he could celebrate it on the 4th—though he declared an armistis and issued us rations on the 3rd." This move was not lost on the besieged residents of Vicksburg, most of whom had not supported secession, because until 1945, the city refused to officially celebrate Independence Day on the Fourth of July.

Neither did Cribbs mention, as did eyewitness Alexander St. Clair Abrams,[69] that when thousands of Rebels marched sullenly and silently to stack their arms, there was no exultation, no cheering from the prevailing Union side, but merely a sharing of haversacks on the part of the victor. Outside of the city, Confederate troops were rounded up and marched into Vicksburg, to await papers for parole and further orders.

69. Harwell, Richard B., ed. *The Confederate Reader* (New York: Dorset Press, 1992), p. 206.

Not wishing to tie up the Union transportation system by sending the estimated 30,000 Confederates to Northern prison camps, Grant decided to parole them, assuming naively that the weary defenders would be fed up with fighting and go back to their homes where they would be a drain on the Southern economy.

After a week of waiting, 24,000 remnant Rebels, defeated and unarmed, marched away from eight months of strife and sacrifice. They felt shattered, humiliated, and mournful. The 20th Alabama Infantry made the long walk of defeat across Mississippi to parole camp at Demopolis, Alabama, to await a prisoner exchange for Union soldiers also in captivity. Perhaps this is the source of Cribb's sense of being exchanged for Union German-American soldiers under General Franz Sigel's command. (Recall that Cribbs had claimed that 15,000 German prisoners under Franz Sigel were freed in exchange for Confederates.) Since neither the North nor the South could handle all the prisoners taken, exchanges were made early in the war. When the policy was discontinued because parolees reenlisted for the fight, prison camps became death camps of disease and starvation for both South and North factions.

Marching Back to Tennessee

With the death of General Garrott during the siege of Vicksburg, newly promoted General Pettus took his command. The exchange of prisoners set the Alabama Brigade back into the fray less than two months after surrender. General Pettus was ordered to march the exchanged Alabama Brigade north to reinforce General Bragg in western Tennessee, near Knoxville.

Cribbs wrote this account of what happened next:

We were soon placed in posission on Lookout Mountain engaging Genl Hooker for several hours. Our ammunition gave out and the Yanks were crowding us. We prised up Boulders and rolled them down the mountain onto them and did them more damage than our Minnies did.

We were relieved about 12 oclock that night, marched to the foot of the mountain to Missionary Ridge, slept three or four hours, got breakfast, and marched up the ridge to the Georgia RR [Rail Road] Tunnell where Genl Sherman's Division attacted our line soon after we got in position, charging our posission repeatedly till about five oclock P.M. when they drew off and our line was formed in a Hollow Square, guarde against Cavelry. Our center line had given way and Genl Bragg was retreating and our Brigade was held as rear guard.

We moved off about dark, arriving at the river finding the bridge burnt. Our men fording the river which was about three feet deap—and ice forming on each bank. It was surely cold. I think this was the Chicamanga [Chickamanga] River, and about midnight. I was taken with pneumonia and left at a private house. I was near dead. Too sick to be moved.

When the Spring Campain opened, Brigade Surgeon and Genl Pettus visited me and advised me to resigne, that I would never be able for active duty again. I was 2nd Lieutenant of my company. There was but little hope for my recovery. I resigned and was sent to Atlanta, Georgia with the Sick and Wounded. I remained in Atlanta till the Spring Campaign opened and our army was falling back. I was sent to Montgomery, Alabama where I remained till about the lst of June, improving slowly. I proceeded on to my home near Tuscaloosa, Alabama.

I continued to improve slowly. Being annoyed by the Conscript Officer, he wanted to send me to the conscript camp. I objected, but proposed to go to my old Co. as a Private. He objected, so I sliped off to Selma and was detailed on Post Duty in the commissary Department where I remained till December 22nd. My Father wrote to me Capt. Slaughter (the Conscript Officer) was hunting for me and would likely make trouble for me.

There were quite a few of Genl Forrests men there for the winter and some of them were staying with him and it would be best for me to come home and enlist with them. I enlisted, joining Capt Pages Co. of the 15 & 16 Kentuckey Cavelry, commanded by Col. Chinnaworth [Thomas J. Chenoweth] who were at my Fathers and who said they would protect me from Capt. Slaughter. Capt. Page had papers for the arrest of Capt. Slaughter, so when Capt Slaughter arrested me, Capt. Page arrested him and sent him to Montgomery and sent him to his command.

While Cribbs was dealing with an overzealous conscription officer, the 20th Alabama Infantry Regiment had withdrawn from the Atlanta Campaign and returned to Tennessee for the Battle of Nashville, leaving General William T. Sherman little opposed in his burn and pillage March to the Sea. Not ready to give up, the Confederates marched to North Carolina for a showdown near the coast at Kinston and Bentonville. The Union forces found little organized opposition in the heartland of the South, so General James Wilson and his Cavalry Corps, armed with seven-shot repeating rifles, were sent to lead raids.

Their mission was to destroy Alabama's industries and, particularly, the arsenal and arms manufacturing facility at Selma. Opposing were the less organized and scattered Confederate Cavalry led by General Nathan Bedford Forrest. Ultimately, Wilson's Raids captured five fortified cities, 288 cannons, 6,820 prisoners, and captured Confederate President Jefferson Davis near Irwinville, Georgia.[70] Cribbs wrote this about the conflict:

> I was in active service again, and when the Spring Campaign opened up, Genl Forrest got on Genl Willsons raid and headed him off south of Huntsville, Alabama. Lyons' Kentuckey Brigade [Union] attacted them at the Mile Creek near Centerville [Centreville], Alabama. I was captured again, just a day before Genl Lee's surrender, and was taken on to Montgomery, Alabama and on towards Tuskeega [Tuskegee], Alabama. I was parolled near Tuskeega several days after being captured. This is my army record as near as I can remember it. As I stated I am shy on dates.[71]

With Cribbs slowly recuperating from pneumonia taken after his crossing of the freezing Chickamauga River, he was sent to Atlanta. The 20th Alabama Infantry went into winter camp at Dalton, Georgia. His comrades became engaged in a heated contest to defend Atlanta, where they were conspicuous at Rocky Face but lost heavily at Kennesa and Jonesboro, where they faced the hail of iron.

Their severe losses and subsequent retreat opened the way for the Union's near "total war" of destruction by General Sherman, sweeping across Georgia. Meanwhile, the 20th Alabama remnant marched back into Tennessee with General Hood. Losing severely at Nashville, they left the disastrous field and marched over the

---

70. "Wilson's Raid," Wikipedia, https://en.wikipedia.org/wiki/Wilson%27s_Raid. Accessed 2/24/2022.

71. Cribbs, Philander A. Pension file reproduced from the holdings of the Texas State Archives, Motley County Museum, Matador, Texas.

Cumberland Gap into North Carolina. Near the coast they fought and lost at Kinston and participated in the last tactical offense of the Confederates at Bentonville. From that disastrous final battle, the 165 rank and file of the 20th Infantry marched to Salisbury, North Carolina, to lay down their arms in surrender on March 19, 1865.[72]

As evidenced by his own words and those of other eyewitnesses to events that touched him, Philander Cribbs experienced firsthand many of the innovations and strategies of a modern war. Although there is no direct mention of railroads, telegraph, newspapers, or photography, their importance in the defeat of Cribbs' allies cannot be overstated. Among the new strategies employed by both sides were flanking maneuvers as opposed to frontal assaults, the cavalry as counter-intelligence agents and guerrillas, effective mobilization by marching fast without supporting supply lines, the use of interior lines to deploy troops and artillery, the blockades of the waterways, and control of the rivers and ports by gunboats and ironclads.

"Modern" innovations aside, the common foot soldier marched thousands of thankless miles to face death standing in a hollow square against oncoming cavalry, or fighting germs in a camp or prison to overcome measles or dysentery. Out of the original 1,100 men of the 20th that engaged in battle for the Confederacy, only 63 were present on that day of surrender.[73]

P.A. Cribbs survived despite the ungodly carnage of a bloody civil war that killed or wounded six out of ten of his fellow Confederates. Despite the scanty rations and hardships of living outdoors in all kinds of weather; despite sieges, assaults, and pursuit

---

72. "Twentieth Alabama Infantry Regiment." https://archives.alabama.gov/referenc/ alamilor/20thinf.html. Created: 11/26/96. Accessed 2/24/2022.

73. "Twentieth Alabama Infantry Regiment." https://archives.alabama.gov/referenc/ alamilor/20thinf.html. Created: 11/26/96. Accessed 2/24/2022.

by a conscription officer; despite the ordeal of being captured, by his count, three times; and despite the long march that would take his unit across six states and far beyond 3,000 miles, P.A. Cribbs survived.

According to the family history, "In his later years Phy often spent the winter months in warmer climes. It was not uncommon to see him lolling on Redondo Beach in his swim suit or tripping the light fantastic in the 49ers Club at San Bernadino, [California]."[74]

After review by the Office of the Adjunct General of the U.S. War Department, the pension for Philander A. Cribbs was reinstated,[75] but it was not to last long. His short winter visits to climates warmer than those frigid camps on long marches would soon cease. Just months after his pension's renewal, Cribbs passed away on March 6, 1927, in temperate San Antonio, where he attained the age of 90 years, 8 months, and 9 days.

Apparently, the pneumonia damage that Cribbs suffered in the Civil War plagued him for the rest of his life. His infirmity saved him from participating in some of the last desperate battles of the war, but it drove him to work his daughters like unpaid servants. Before making any judgments on such a man, take a walk, a long walk, in his shoes.

---

74. Traweek, Eleanor. "P. A. Cribbs Family," *Of Such as These: A History of Motley County* (Quanah, Texas: Nortex, 1976), p. 223.

75. Cribbs Family File. Records of the Adjutant General's Office of the U.S. War Department, Washington, D.C., Motley County Museum, Matador, Texas.

The Long March for the Confederacy
20th ALABAMA REGIMENT, INFANTRY

1. Tuscaloosa, ALA — Co. K Volunteers – 13 Sept. 1861
2. Mobile, ALA — Training – Nov 1861
3. Knoxville, TN — Cumberland Gap - 18 June 1862
4. Frankfort, KY — Chickasaw Bayou – 27 Dec. 1862
5. Port Gibson, MISS — Port Gibson – 1 May 1863
6. Vicksburg, MISS — Vicksburg Surrender – 3 July 1863
7. Demopolis, ALA — Patrol Camp Detention – 8 July 1863
8. Chattanooga, TN — Chattanooga Siege – Sept. & Nov 1863
9. Atlanta, GA — Atlanta Campaign – May to Sept. 1864
10. Nashville, TN — Retreat and Regroup – Oct. 1864
11. Kinston, NC — Carolinas Campaign – Feb. to Apr. 1865
12. Bentonville, NC — Last Tactical Battle for CAS – 19 Mar. 1865
13. Salisbury, NC — Final Surrender: April 9, 1865

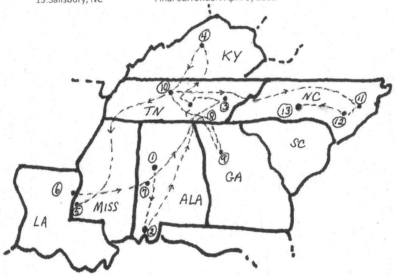

Map of the route Cribbs' unit walked during his time in the infantry

The Letters:
Correspondence Between D. C. Kieth and Ella E. Cribbs

The original "period" letters offered here as typed versions were often faded, difficult to read, and required some interpretation.

A minimum amount of editing and added punctuation was used only when necessary to clarify meaning. Original spelling, capitalization, and most punctuation was retained.

December 12, 1886
(No envelope remains for postmark)

From: Dockum
Dickens Co. Texas
Dec. 12 1886

To: Miss Ella Cribs.

Unknown Miss. It is with pleasure I take the privlidge of writing to you asking you to corospond with me as I wish to corospond with you. Miss Ella a friend of yours recommended you to me.

From an unknown,
D.C. Kieth

Feb. 2, 1887
(Postmark: _NYDE_ , _EXA_ [Snyder, Texas])

To: Miss Ella Cribbs
Ft. Spunky PO
Hood County, Texas

From: Dockum
Dickens Co., Texas
Jan. 29 1887

To: Miss Ella Cribbs,

Absent friend. I take the gratest of pleasure in trying to answer your kind and welcom letter wich came to hand the 16th. I can say that I certainly red your letter with much pleasure. Miss Ella I am glad to know you air wiling to hold a corrospondents with me. You will find me very dull and a very poor scribe though I am wiling to do my best.

You ask me to remember you to your friend that gave me your address. He isent in this countrie now though I gess he will be heare next Spring. He is thought of as a very nice young man in this countrie. Though I haven't known him very long my self.

I suppose you would like to know what I follow and a bout what kind of man I am. I am twenty five years of age and light complected and a small man. The work I follow is with cattle. I am only a poor lonely western cow boy.

I know cow boys has a verry wild name a noung most of people, though I don't think I am of a wild disperzision. They is a grate many cow boys that isent half as wild as their names. I have been running cattle five years. I came to this countrie from Jacksbo with a hird of my uncles cattle five years ago. I am from Tennessee to Texas. I have a grate many relaties [relatives] living in Texas though I haven't any in this countrie atal.

It is a grate pleasure to a young man in this countrie to read a letter from a kind Ladie friend. They isent very many Ladies in this countrie though we manage to have a dance once and a while. Do you dance or air you a church member? I like to dance my self though it is very seldom I ever get to go to a dance.

Please excuse writing and misspells words. I will close for this time. Sending my best regards to you. Write soon and often to your unknown friend.

D.C. Kieth

March 9, 1887
(Postmark: [Dick]ens, [Texas])

To: Miss Ella Cribbs
Ft. Spunky, Hood County Texas

From: Dockum
Dickens Co. Texas
March 6 1887

To: Miss Ella Cribbs

Kind friend. I take much pleasure in trying to answer your kind and welcom letter wich reached me the 26th of last month. I hope you will not think strange of me for not writing sooner. This is the first chance I have had to write since I received your letter. I had to leave the ranch a few days before your letter came and it was sent to me. I am always from the ranch now on a work and don't know when I will be back. I haave a poar chance to write out with the wagon.

You wanted to know if I had any realties [relatives] living in that part of the State, not as I know of. They is some Keiths [sic] living in Erath County though I don't think they aire any kin to me. You can see the difference in the way we spell our names.

Miss Ella, I would like very much to have one of your pictures, if you will send me one I will take good ceare of it and return it if you evr call for it. When you see our friend agan give him my regards and tell him I hope he will come back to this countrie this spring.

They was a dance in this countrie a ew nights ago a bout five miles from whaire we was campt. I dident attend the dance my self thogh all the rest of the boys went.

We aire having some very pretty weather and out heare now and the little coullies is getting greean once more. Well, I will halft to close for this time. Hoping you will excuse this short and dull letter. Your known and tru friend.

D.C. Kieth

P.S. Please write soon and often. Good By.

Mar 18, 1887

(No envelope or postmark)

[The valentine in the original letter shows a hand holding a large horseshoe filled with flowers, framing a snow-covered scene, the bare trees and birds feeding. A building in the far background is surrounded by violets and bell-shaped white flowers, while a banner proclaims: "Flowers of Friendship."]

Valentine
May happiness & Prosperity ever be thy lot.

From: Ft. Spunky
Mar 18 1887
To: D.C. Kieth

I received your kind letter 15th inst. Although I looked for it two mails sooner. We live one mi. from the P. O. & mails come and go twice a week. I am & will be verry lonely this spring as sister Maggie commenced teaching school last Monday. Sister Carrie our baby sister is going to her. Pa & Dan our only brother is working in the field, there-fore Ma & I have to keep house almost alone. I much rather work in the house than in the field, though I have to do both.

I am invited to a party at my brother-inlaw's to night. It seems like the people never get tired to dancing. I don't dance, though they never fail to send me an invitation. I have not saw Mr. Meriman since I wrote to you last. He lives in a neighbor-hood about 7 mi. from ours.

I will send you one of my pictures in my next letter in exchange for one of yours. Believing you will be as good as your word in regard of returning it. As for taking care of it I cant say it is worthy of much protection.

You must plant a garden or a melon patch for it will make a good scarescrow to help the intruders off. Please excuse my nonsense. You & your friend Mr. Jenkins must come down next summer & enjoy the protracted meetings & other gatherings with us, as that is the farmers holiday, I believe. We also have Sunday school every Sunday. And a very interesting literary society every Saturday night. We have not had a good season since the 19 of last June. Therefore, the farmers are very much discouraged & some have left their homes & are gone to the railroad. Do the people ever farm any where you live & is it very seasonable out there?

Would it be asking to much for your name in full? Please excuse my inquisitiveness & this [poorly] written & composed letter. Write soon & a long letter to your faithful friend.

Ella Cribbs

Mar. 22, 1887

(Handwritten postmark on envelope: Ft. Spunky Tex   Mar 22/87; two postmarks on back of envelope: Colo[rado City?], Texas & Cl[eburn?], Tex)

[At the top of this letter, very much like the one written on March 18, is a Valentine with the illustration of a house by a stream and mountains, surrounded by flowers and a banner "Forget me not."
By lifting the valentine, these words are revealed:
"May happiness and prosperity ever be thy lot. Ella."]

To: Mr. D.C. Kieth
Dockum Ranch
Dickens Co. Texas

From: Ft. Spunky Texas
Mar 20 1887
To: Mr. D.C. Kieth

    I patiently waited for your kind letter which came in last Tuesdays mail (though I looked for it sooner) & was glad to hear from you. We live one mi. from Ft. Spunky & the mails come & go twice a week.

    We are having quite a continued drouth, we havnt had a good season since the 18th of last June. The farmers are very much discouraged though some have planted corn & some have planted corn & some have left their farms & gone to the rail-road to work. And some are not doing any thing, waiting for it to rain. Is it very seasonable in your part of the country & is there any farms out there?

    I am & will be very lonely this spring as Sister Maggie commenced teaching school last Monday. There is only 5 of us children. I have 2 sisters & one brother younger than my self. Sister Maggie is the eldest. Ma & I have to keep house almost alone. I had much rather work in the house than in the field though I have done both. I attened a party at my brother-inlaw's last Friday night. I don't dance my self though we never fail to get an invitation.

    I have not saw Mr. Merriman since I wrote to you last. It is about 7 mi. from our neighborhood to where he lives. When I saw him he said he was going to start soon for the ranch. I will send you one of my pictures in my next in exchang for one of yours. Believing you will be as good as your word in regard of returning it. As for taking care of it, I cant say it is worthy of much protection.

You & your friend Mr. Jenkins must come down next summer & enjoy the protracted meetings & other gatherings with us, as that is a farmers holiday I believe. We have Sunday school every Sunday morning & singing in the afternoon & preaching three times a month, and a very interesting spelling match evry Saturday night.

Would it be asking to much for your name in full, please excuse my inquistivness & this badly written & composed letter. Write soon & a long letter to your faithful friend.

Ella Cribbs

Mar [27], 1887

(Postmark: Dockum Ranch, Texas; this time D.C. signs his full name, fulfilling her previous requests in two different letters.)

To: Miss Ella Cribbs
Ft. Spunky
Hood County Texas

From: Dockum Texas
March 27 1887

To: Miss Ella Cribbs.

Absent friend your kind and most welcome letter reached me yesterday. It was red with ceare and much pleasure. I am glad to know you air willing to send me your picture though am sorrow I haven't one of mine to send to you. Though I will promis you that I will have one taken the first chance and send it to you. I don't know when I will get the chance to have one taken as I live so far from any town.

You wanted to know if this was a seasonable countrie. Not very. It hasent rained in this part of the countrie for several months. Though I don't wonder at it not raining in a cow countrie for they work Sunday as well as any other day, though it is most imposible for a cow man to tend to his bisness unless he works on Sunday. They is some few farms in this countrie though the most of them air ranch farms, rais[ing] mostley hay for the horses in the winter. I don't think this countrie will ever bee much of a farming countrie.

Our friend Mr. Merriman is in this countrie now though I haven't saw him since he returned. I haven't saw Mr. Jenkins since last January. I met him one day on my line and had quite a talk with him. Are you acquainted with Mr. Jenkins? He doesn't know that I am correspond[ing] with you unless some one has told him. I think a gradeal of Mr. Jenkins. He seams to bee a very nice young man.

Miss Ella, I am sorrow to think you will bee so lonsome this spring. I wish I could meet you and talk with you. I think I would injoy my self with you. You have no ida how much I appreciate reading your letters. If you should fail to get an answer from me to any of your letters this summer for some time, you will please not get offended as I am liable to bee off on a cow hunt and not get your letter for several days.

I will close for this time sending my regards to you. Write soon and often to your tru and faithful friend.

Daniel Crofford Kieth

[Apr] 29, 1887

(Postmark: [Clebur]ne Tex.)

To: Mr. D.C. Kieth
Dockums Ranch
Dickens Co. Tex.

From: Ft. Spunky
April 28, 1887
To: Mr. D.C. Kieth
Dockums Ranch

I received your kind missive some time since & would have answered it sooner but have been very busy since it rained (we had a good rain the 16 instant) helping Pa replant his corn. I also planted a pea-nut patch. The farmers are very backward with their crop this year, though the spring is late. I trust evry person will make plenty this year.

I have joined the Farmers Aliance since I wrote to you, also attended a meeting last night. There were 9 ladies [initiated] when I joined & one joined last night. It is the only secret society that I am a member of.

I will send my Photo as I promised & will look for yours by return mail. You can see by looking at my picture that you are corresponding with a very homely & rustic girl. I trust that my daily life will excell my photo.

For the deeds done here in the flesh is what we will be judged by when we all appear before the judgment bar of <u>Christ</u>. Our Sunday school & singing is very interesting. Sister Maggie is the ladies first Bible class teacher & I am the second Bible class teacher. I would rather be a scholar than teacher. I should not complain when we have a duty to perform.

You ask if I was acquainted with Mr Jenkins. I am not though I obtained his where-a-bouts through other parties. As he don't know that we are corresponding, perhaps he would not like for unknown friends to betray him. As ladies are accused of telling every thing they know any way. I trust that I have not done any harm by using his name. Do you think he will be angry with me?

How come Mr Merriman to give you my address & why did he reccommend me when he, I expect, had other friends that would be more interesting. Please excuse my inquisitiveness, for you may have other friends made by his kindness.

I am glad to know my letters are appreciated by you & hope they will help you to while away the lonely hours if nothing more. I imagine that a frontier life is very rough & lonely. I would like to meet you in the near future, though I am not verry intertaining. I will close for fear my letter will fall in the hands of intruders in your absents.

Give my respects to Mr. Merriman. Write soon & a long letter to your absent & unknown friend.

Ella Cribbs.

[May] 9, [1887]

(Postmark illegible)

To: Miss Ella Cribbs
F.T. Spunky
Hood Co. Texas

From: Dockum Ranch Texas
May 6 1887
To: Miss Ella Cribbs

Kind friend. I take much pleasure in attempting to answer your kind and most welcome letter wich came to hand yesterday. Miss Ella I am very much pleased with your photograph. Though I am sorrow that I haven't one of mine to send you though I will bee as good as my promis I will send you one the first chance I have to have some taken. I don't expect I will have any chance to get any photos taken before I go Home.

I expect I will go home some time next winter. Whair I call my home is at my sisters [Sophronia Kieth Garner] in Jack county. I haven't been to see my people in three years so I think I shall go to see them next winter if nothing hapons more than I am expecting.

Miss Ella, dont think that you hirt any ones feealings by speaking of Mr Jenkins, for you did not. You wanted to know why Mr Meriman give me your address. I ask him last faul if he dident have some young ladi friend he could give me hir address to write to. So he sed he did and gave me your address and spoke with a grate respect of you and sed you was a good friend of his. Though I hadent known Mr Meriman but a short time. I am not acquainted with but a few young Ladies in the State. You air the only Ladi friend I corospond with, that is your Lady friend. Though you can tell from my letter I am a new hand at the bisness.

Please excuse this short and badley written letter. Miss Ella, I commence my letter this morning and I will half to finish with a different pen and ink. I was at the store when I commence my letter. So I will try to finish it this earning, and as I have time this earning I will write more than I expected I would get to write. I am a poor hand to write though I had much rather do my own writing than to have some one else to write for me.

Mr Meriman and my self works in the branding outfit on the range. We have been working very hard for the last three weeks geathern hirds for the trail. We have got two hirds ready to start now and when they leave we will half to go to geathern another one, then when it gets off we will go to branding calves.

I seean Mr Jenkins a few days ago and had quite a talk with him. He is much liv[li]er then my self. I like to bee with him. I told him that you spoke a bout us coming down next summer. He sed he wish it was so we could go, and so I wish so two. Though I gess it will bee most imposible. I know you will get tired trying to read this badley written letter so I will close for the present by sending you my best regards. Write soon and often to your unknown friend.

D.C. Kieth.

Jun 16, 1887

(Hand-cancelled postmark, crest embossed on notepaper)

Jayton Tex
To: Miss Ella Cribbs
F. T. Spunky
Hood County, Texas

From: Dockums
Dickens Co. Texas
June 13 1887

To: Miss Ella Cribbs

Absent friend. I take grate pleasure in trying to answer your kind letter I received the 9ᵗʰ. I was so glad to hear from you but was sorrow to hear you had to work so hard. I am not working in the branding outfit now I am cow hunting on the out side. I haven't seean Mr Meriman for over a month. I was at his outfit yesterday but only staied a few minutes. I am out on a hunt now. I gess I will not get to go to the ranch any more for some time. I hope you will have a nice time this summer going to the getherns around. I hope you will think of your tru friend in the west the Saturday before the forth of July. I am shure I will think of you if I am living. I wish I could get to come down thair this summer though I gess it will bee impossible for me to come this summer. I will come to see you next faul when I start home if it will bee agreeable with you.

Miss Ella, you have no ida how glad I would bee if I could see you. I think I would injoy your company so much. Please don't think I will dseave you in sending you my picture for I will send you one the first chance. I think so much of your picture and your letters, I know I would think a greadeal of you. You ask me how the

Prohibition question was with the people in this countrie. I haven't hird but very little sed a bout it though I am in hopes they will do away with whiskey altogether. You will please excuse short letter and I will try and do better the next one. The grass and water is fine and stock looks well. Miss Ella, please alow me to ask you why you wanted to know my name in full.

Mr. Meriman's brother is working on this ranch. I only seean him once. Tell Miss Maggie that Mr. J. C. is liable to get killed [since] Espuela Company has got him turning trail hurd round thaire pasture. Some of them air very hard to turn. Well, it is very near night and I haft to go a good ways to camps. So I will close by asking you to write soon and often.

Your tru friend as ever, Good By.

D.C. Kieth

[Continuation of June 16, 1887 postmark]

June 15 1887

To: Miss Ella Cribbs

I rote to you the 13 th and was in such rush I dident get to say all I wish to say. So as I have time this earning I will write you a few more lins. Please eaxcuse pencil as it is all I have to write with now. You wanted to know if my pairents was living. I have one Sister [Sophronia Kieth Garner] and one Brother [Charles Bledsoe Kieth]. They aire bouth older than my self. They aire bouth mairred, one living in Texas and one living in Tenn. My Sister livs in Jack Co., that is whaire I call my home. I haven't ben home in three years so I think I shall go next winter if nothing happens more than I am expecting. I have ben lonely to day but we haven't done anything but kill a beaf and look after our horses. Though I gess we will comens work in the morning and I knot know when we will get to rest agan. I hope youal aire blessed with good rains by this time. The grass is better in this countrie at this time than has been for three years before.

Miss Ella, I know that it looks better for a young man to send his photo first. Though it will not cause me to think any the less of you. It made me think more of you to know you was kind a enough to send me yours first after I explained why I couldent send my photo first. You spoke a bout the people saying they though[t] all the young Ladies of that county would bee mairred before the year was out. I hope it will not turn out to be so for I would hate to heare of you mairrien as I injoy corresponding with you so much. I told Mr Meriman you must bee the best Girl in the world from the letters you wrote and he sed you was. I am glad to think you think a nough of me to offer a praier for me. May the lord bless you and bee with you to the end. Your tru and faithful friend. Good By.

D.C. Kieth

July 23, 1887

(No postmark stamp, hand-cancelled with X)

Jayton Tex

To: Miss Ella Cribbs
Fort Spunky
Hood County Tex

From: Jayton PO
Kint [Kent] Co. Tx
July 18 1887

To: Miss Ella Cribbs.

Kind and tru friend. I received your kind and most welcome letter the 12ᵗʰ. I read it with much pleasure as I do all of your letters. I hope you will forgive me for not answern sooner. I have quit the Espuela Company and working for the TO Company. This Company pay[s] me more than I was getting. This ranch is 25 miles southeast of the Espuela ranch.

I havent sean Mr Meriman since last spring, that was about the 8th of May. I think he is still working in the branding outfit. I sean Mr. J. C. a few days ago. He sed give his regard to Miss Maggie. Miss Ella, I think I can send you my photo some time in September, if I can possibly I will do so. They is a young Man stays here that is interested in the company, taks photos, but hasent his instruments out hear. So he ses he will have them hear some time this summer. Though the longer I put off sending my photo to you I expect the better it will bee for me. For I expect when you get it, you will send it back and send for yours. You spoke a bout starting school and ask me if I thought I could rejoice with you. I cirtanly think I can.

Have youal had any rain since you written to me last. I hope you have. It is getting very dry out hear now and very warm. I am so glad that my cow hunting is over until faul. I haven't nothing to do now except wride a round the beaf pasture evry day. That is only a short wride theas long days. I can start in the morning and get in by twelve. I just return to the ranch the 12th of this month from a cow hunt.

When I am out on a cow hunt I generly haft to wride all day and then gard the cattle at neight. I don't mean that I gard them all neight my self for they is generly 10 or 12 of us to gether and we take time a bout garding them at neight. So you can imagine how taired a pirson would get working neight and day for a month at the time.

You wanted to know if we all wouldent like to live in a thicker settled countrie. I can speak for my self. Yes, I had much rather if I was fixed like I want to bee. I know I am a poor Man and half to work for a living, and I can get more for my work in this countrie than I could in a farming countrie. I would like to bee fix some day so I could live in the settlement and have a home of my own. I hope that I will bee fix some day so that I wont half to depend upon wages for a living. I think a pirson would bee better satisfied if they had a little home of thaire own and could make thaire living at home. I expect to have a home some day if I live to bee very old and have good luck.

So far as me leaving my home and coming out west to sow my wild oats. I can expalin my part of it to you. This countrie is as much home as I have got, though I call my sister' home. Though you air about wright in the way you spoke about young men learning their home and goint over the world to sow their wild oats.

Miss Ella, please allow me to ask you your age as I don't think you told me how old you was. Youer photo looks to bee about 17.

We have some very fine plums out heare now and it is only a bout fifty yards from the hous to the plum patch. I expect I had better bring my letter to a close for I know you will get tired reading such a scribbled and [badly] composed letter as this. In the way you spoke a bout a cow boys life is just a bout wright. I am glad to know you had a nice time the Saturday before the 4th of July. I had a nice time at a round up working hard all day and garding the cattle that neight. I thought of you and wondered if you wasent having a nice time. I wish I could have been thaire to injoyed my self with you and your friends.

They is three of us staying hear at this ranch now. One milks and one cooks and I wride the beaf pasture. I haven't wriden it today. Will half to wride it this earing. I stayed at the ranch this morning a purpos to write to you. We have lots of checkens and eggs at this ranch and we also have a patch of corn and irish potatos and a plum py evry once and a while. We aire not the best of cooks in the world but we do the best we can.

Miss Ella, why do you think of living an old maid. Do you prefear that kind of life. I had rather think a married life would bee a much happier life.

I will close for this time hoping you will excuse this badly written letter. Write soon to your tru friend.

D.C. Kieth.

[August 9, 1887]

(No postmark stamp; stamp torn; handwritten: Ft. Spunky Tex)

To: D.C. Kieth
King Co. (Jayton PO) Tex

From: Ft. Spunky Hood Co.
Aug 8 1887

To: Mr. D.C. Kieth

Kind sir. Your kind and highly appreciated letter came O.K. the [31]st inst. I was glad to heare you was well & doing well. That is more than we can say. There is a great deel of sickness here for it to be so dry. My mother have been in bad health all this year.

The drouth ended last night with a glorious rain, but too late to make corn. We planted 20 acres in corn & I don't expect we will make the seed we planted. Some of our neighbors have done gathered their corn crop & a meal sack would hold it all. I don't know what will become of us, all times distressing. I don't believe the Lord will let us suffer, if we will only trust him. However, we will live in hope if we die in dis-pair.

Pa says he will try this country one more year, as he cant get away this year. We have been trying to go to Washington Territory for the last three years, but have failed. I expect we are to [choose] any way. The "Bible says" contentment, with Godliness is great gain. I have long since made up my mind to be satisfied with my lot where ever it may be cast. There is some pleasure living when a person can be composed & satisfied.

I attened the wedding I spoke of in my last letter & was a [waiter]. There was 2 more weddings last Sunday but did not attend either of them. I also attened a Prohibition speaking & picnic lately. I believe the Anti's side was the victory. That is the last news we had. I am very sorry as I was on the other side. I always want my side to win, but we don't always get evry thing our way. I am very well pleased going to school. It will be out in 3 weeks, and we will have an examination then.

Don't forget to go to see your sister next winter & to see us. I have one dear sister married [Lillie Cribbs Thompson] & I always like to go to see her. I am sorry your parents are dead, though we all will have to give them up some day & our best friends to. I have been blest with good parents so far, & am thankful for them. I may have to part from them someday. We cant live together here always, but we can in Heaven.

You ask why I spoke about being an old maid. I don't expect to be one if I can help it, for old maids like old bachelors' have to ware a hard name. That don't make any difference, though I would not like to be called a dispisable old maid. I may have to ware that name yet, as the poet says, "They are all getting married but me." My friends tell me I am to hard to please, but I don't think so.

I would like to keep house for some nice young man, as keeping house is one of my greatest cares. I don't expect I could do my duty but would try as hard as any person. You ask how old I am. I was 20 years old when I had the picture taken I sent you. I was 22 years old the 27th of last Oct. I would like to have a complete dis-scription of your self if a greeable. I will look for your picture soon. Then I will see how good looking you are.

I expect you are tired of my ugly picture by this time. I can agree with you in regard to working for wages & as you spoke about having a home. I have always heard it where was a will, there was a way. I must close. Write soon to your friend.

Ella Cribbs.

Aug 23, 1887

(No postmark, hand cancelled with X; handwritten: Jayton Tex)

Miss Ella please forgive me for saying you [come] to be an old maid. I was mistaken in the way your letter red when I written to you last. I am so sorrow I made such remark to you. If you will forgive me I will be so glad. So far as getting tired of your photo I never will. I only hope you will think as much of mine as I do of yours.

Miss Ella we know nothing a bout each other only by reputations. Though your letters satisfies me that you aire one among the best Girls in the world. I will describe my self the best I can. My age is 25. I will bee 26 years old the 7th of next October. My weight is 145 lbs. I am also light complected and gray eyes.

How do you think you would like to keep house In the west for a cow boy. I would like to have a nice young ladie to keep house for me. I wouldent bee able to live in a very fine house though I would treat hir as well as I was able to.

I will tell you why I quit the Espuela outfit. They dont alow their men to buy cattle. I bought a bunch of cattle last spring and went to the Ranch and quit for I new if I dident quit they would turn me off this faul. Though this outfit had already told me they would give me $30 dolars per month and work the year round and let me hold my cattle with them.

Don't think I am telling you this to try to make you believe I am worth verry much for I am not. I have always had a good living and I always expect to have if I can have it by living [h]onest. I believe as long as a pirons liv an [h]onest life they will prosper some way or nother. I will close for this time by sending my regards and best wishes to youal. Your tru friend.

D.C. Kieth.

Nov. 9, 1887

Jayton, Tex.

To: Miss Ella Cribbs.
F.T. Spunky
Hood County, Texas.

From: Jayton PO Kent Co. Tx.
Nov 3 1887

To: Miss Ella Cribbs.

Absent friend. You[r] kind and most welcom letter of the 21st of October was [first] received from you since Augst. I left the Ranch the 29th of Augst on a cow hunt and returned the 18th of October and found no letter from you. Though they was a letter sent down whaire I was at work for me, but I dident get it. Probly it was your letter. It will be sent back to me the first chance.

When I got to the Ranch I stayed two days and then started to Colorado City with a hurd of beaf cattle. So I returned a gan the first and will start out a gan tomorror to be gone a bout 10 days, and then I think I will be done cow hunting for this year. I received the papers you sent me, though I havent had time to read them. I will read them this winter at neights. I put them all a way in my trunk. I am very thankfull to you for them.

I am sorrow to know that you haft to work so hard. I hope you may live to see the day you can live with out doint hard work. I expect to stay in this countrie two or three years longer, if I live that long. I hope I may be able by that time to go east and settle down. I don't think I could ever make up my mind to settle in this countrie. Though I like to live hear and like the people but I don't think this will ever bee much of a farming countrie. I have got my mind made up to mairrie when I am 30 years of age, if I would live to bee that old provided I can. We have had some very cool weather in this countrie this faul. They is plent of water every whairs but little grass.

[Miss Ella, I think if I could see you pirsionly, [would] think a gradeal of you though it is not nessearly for eather of us to alow our selvs to think any more of one another than friends. I can say one thing, that I never corrosponded with a young lady that I injoyed reading hir letters better than I do yours. Why I write the way I have written I think it would bee very foolish in me to alow my self to think any more of you only as a good friend. I suppose you live in a thick setted countrie whaire they is lots of nice young men. I know any of them would bee glad to get as good and as nice of young lady as I think you air.

If I ever leave this countrie on a pleasur trip I am coming to see you provided you air still single. I though[t] last spring I would get to take a trip this winter though it will bee most impossible for me to do so. I find your hair is about the color of my mothers hair though you aire some heaver than she was. Hir wait was 95 and 100. She generly waid 95 in the summer and 100 in the winter.

I will bring my letter to a close as it is late at neight and I haft to get up early and start on a cow hunt. I send my regards to youal. Write soon to your tru and faithful friend.

D.C. Kieth. Good Neight.

Nov 18, 1887

(No envelope; contains a valentine card: "May happiness & Prosperity ever be thy lot.")

From: Ft. Spunky, Tex
Nov 18, 1887

To: Mr. D.C. Kieth

I received your kind letter 15th inst. Although I looked for it two mails sooner. We live one mi. from the P.O. & mails come & go twice a week. I am & will be verry lonly this spring as sister Maggie commenced teaching school last Monday, & sister Carrie our baby sister is going to her. Pa & Dan our only brother is working in the field, therefore Ma & I have to keep house almost alone. I much rather work in the house than in the field, though I have to do both. I am invited to a party at my brother-in-laws to night. It seems like the people never will get tired of dancing. I don't dance, though they never fail to send me an invitation. I have not saw Mr. Meriman since I wrote to you last. He lives in a neighbor-hood about 7 mi. from ours.

I will send you one of my pictures in my next letter, in exchange for one of yours. Believing you will be as good as your word in regard to returning it. As for taking care of it I cant say it is worthy of much protection. You must plant a garden or a melon patch for it will make a good scaracrow to help the intruders off. Please excuse my nonsense.

You & your friend Mr. Jenkins must come down next summer & enjoy the protracted meetings & other gatherings with us, as that is the farmers holiday, I believe. We also have Sunday school evry Sunday. And a very interesting literary society evry Saturday night.

We have not had a good season since the 19th last June. Therefore the farmers are very much discouraged, & some have left there homes & are gone to the rail road. Do the people ever farm any where you live & is it very seasonable out there?

Would it be asking to much for your name in full? Please excuse my inquisitiveness, & this [badly] written & composed letter. Write soon & a long letter to your faithful friend.

Ella Cribbs.

Feb 2, 1888

(Handwritten: Ft. Spunky Texas, 2-17-88; hand cancelled with ///;
envelope decorated with bird eating berries on a branch and one
flying; valentine has a bouquet of roses and a ribbon banner with
"Love"; postmark on back: Sweet Water Mar __ 1888, and marked
out: Jayton and Hotsprings Ark.; forwarded: Dockams Ranch Tex.)

To: Mr. D.C. Kieth
Jayton PO. Kint Co. Texas

Longings,
Feb. 14th 1888

I dream of thee in dewy hours,
I think of thee by day,
I muse upon thy wining powers,
When thou art far away.
I love to live in love with thee,
To walk thy pensive eye,
To linger in thy memory,
To soothe thy bosom's signs.
I fain would have thy love-lit face
Forever turned on me,
Oh, may we not in future trace
One common destiny?
And then together we could tread
Life's flowery fields as one,
Dependant on each other's love,
As earth is on the sun.
Each joy in life would brighter be,
If thou were always near,

And wry sorrow lighter be
If thou wert there to cheer.
So let me linger by thy side,
In love with thee alone,
Should fortune frown or ills betide,
Thy presence would atone,
And blest and happy in thy smiles,
Despite of cross or cure,
I'd pray for rare longevity
Thy hold love to share.[76]

A Valentine from a friend to a friend.

Mar 6, 1888
(Postmark: Jayton Tex.)

To: Miss Ella Cribbs
F. T. Spunky
Hood County, Texas

From: Jayton PO. Kent Co. Tex.
Feb 15 1888

To Miss Ella Cribbs.

Dearest frind. I take grate pleasure in trying to answer your
kind & welcome letter of January the 1ˢᵗ. Miss Ella, I received

76. Taylor, Mrs. Enoch. "Love's Longings" in *A Naughty Biography and Other Poems* (Cincinatti: Robert Clarke Co., 1878).

your letter some time since but havent ben able to ansern you. I
have had a very sore hand though it is very near well now. I hope
you will forgive me for not writing sooner for it is my wright hand
that is sore. They was a week I coundent sleep my hand pains me so.

You spoke of your sisters beaing sick, I hope they air well by
this time. I also hope youal aire well. I hird from Mr. Meriman
& Mr Jenkins two or three weeks ago. They was bouth well &
Very well pleased. Mr. Merriman is in cam[p] with the young
Man that I camped with last winter. He is a mity nice young man.

Miss Ella, you wish me to give you a full discriptition of my
self. I am very wiling to do so as near as I can. I will be 27 years
old the 7th of next Oct. if I should live that long. My weight is this
winter 150 lbs. My weight in summer is generly 143. My hair is
a little darker than yours. My eyes air gray. I am high temperd
& I drink whiskey, though I can controle my self. I am stought and
healthy & have ben all my life.

I will look for a discriptition of your self in next letter. I never
did think I could love a pirson of whom I never saw. But you will
please alow me to say that I love your letters & your name & your
repuitation.

Miss Ella, do you believe that you can think enough of me to
promis me your hand & heart in Matrimonia. I only hope that
you do. I am coming down in March if I can possible get off. I
will let you know for sirtain in next letter.

I sent you a Christmas card from Colrado City. Did you get
it. I gess I will get off the train at Gramberry [Granbury] to get
to Ft. Spunky. If so how far is it from the rail road to whaire you

live. I send my regards & best love to youal. Write soon, your tru & loving friend.

D.C. Kieth.

Ma___ 15, 1888

Haskell Tex.
Fisher, Fisher Co., Texas
If not delievered with 10 days

To: Miss Ella Cribbs
F.T. Spunkey
Hood Co. Texas

EMPTY ENVELOPE

No Date

(No envelope; this page was wrapped around
separate tintypes of Ella and D.C.)

Ella to D.C.

I have no objections to povity for that isn't any disgrace to any one. I think if we have the will to do any thing, we surely will be successful in a few things. As I often heard it said, "Whare there is a will there is a way." I think I have as strong will

& determination as any person. At least I generally accomplish almost evry thing I under-take in the working line.

   I would hate to answer your question in the affirmative now, & when you came we might disside aganst each other. If we should agree to marry how thankful we ought to be to Mr Merriman for introducing us, even by letter. I think him any way, for we have had a pleasant correspondence & I hope it will remain so.

   I will look for you this year. You must write me word before you start so I will know when to look for you. You will have my good wishes through life if we never chance to meet. I heartily wish you & your companions a happy new year. I will close by asking to excuse bad spelling & scribbling. I will promice to do better next time. Write soon & a long letter, to your faraway & true friend.

Ella Cribbs

May 30, [188]8

(Postmark: Dockums Ranch Tex; one page is missing)

To: Miss Ella Cribbs
F. T. Spunkey
Hood County-Texas

   You spoke about Mr. Mearriman treating youal very bad when he was down thair. You must not blame him for I ask him if he saw you & he sed he started over to see youal & met some one & they told him youal wasent at hom, that was the reason he dident come to see youal. I am ashamed to send this letter to you though

I gess I will half to or not send any for seve[r]al days, I hope we will get one anothers letter from now on little regular than we have ben getting them. Will close as I am getting very sleepy. I half to start off early in the morning. Write soon & often to you tru friend.

D.C. Kieth

GoodNeight

Aug 11, [1888]
(Postmark: Dockum Ranch, Tex.)

To: Miss Ella Cribbs
F. T. Spunkey
Hood Co. Tex.

From: Dockums
Dickens Co. Tex.

To: Miss Ella Cribbs

Kind & tru friend I am happy to know that I have the pleasure of addressing you a few more lines. I returned to the ranch to day all O.K. though I half to start out a gan in the morning to be gone a bout 10 days. I don't think I will get to go any whairs this summer, only on cow hunts. Faul hunts will comens the first of September.

The ring I sent after for you has come at last. I mailed it to you this earning. I know you air thinking by this time that I was telling you a storrie a bout sending you a ring. Though I hope you will find that I wasent before many days longer. I do wish I could see you & Miss Maggie & talk with you boath. I think I could injoy your company very much. I am thinking off leaving this countrie some time this faul. For I thin[k] I can do better than I am doing hear. I want you to take the ring I send you as a present from a tru friend.

I hope it will be a nice fit. I don't think hard off you for the question you ask me for I think that is your priviledge to find out all a bout me you can.

Please forgive me for beaing so hasty in proposing. As you sed we know nothing a bout each other only by script & our friends word. When we comens writing to each other I never once though[t] off thinking any thing more off you as a good friend. I haven sean Mr. M since I come. Don't know weather he still aims to go down this summer or not. For my self I don't think I can come this summer. Though the first time I come down in that country any whairs I will shure come to see youal. I will half to close for the present. I send my regards to youal & my love to you.

Write soon & often to your tru & faithful friend.

D.C. Kieth.

Sep 3, 1888

(Postmark: Dockam Tex)

To: Miss Ella Cribbs
F. T. Spunkey
Hood Co. Texas

From: Dockam Texas
Sep 2 1888

To: Miss Ella Cribbs

Absent friend. I received your kind & welcom letter to day. I was glad to hear from you though was sorror to hear off your sister being sick, I hope she is well by this time. I also hope this letter will find youal well & injoying your selvs. I am well though I cant say I am injoying my self very much. Though I don't think I have any wright to grumble as long as I am blest with good health & pleanty to live on.

I have ben gone a few days on a visit a bout fifty miles east off hear. Just returned to the Ranch today. I have ben visiting relativs. I know you will think, well, if he has time to visit relativs it looks like he might take time to visit me. If he thinks as much off me as he maks out like he does. I found them all well except my Aunt. She is never well, though she was as well as common.

The reason I went to see them I quit this company & thought I would quit running cattle for a living. So I went to bid them good by, though I always go to see them evry chance I [get] for they are the only kin I have living any ways clost. So my uncle & Aunt wouldent agree for me to leave. So I will start to work to morrow for the Matador company. They will pay me a little better wages than I was geting hear.

My Aunt made me promis to buy a section off land clost to them & settle down. So I will buy some land in this countrie & settle down & do the best I can. My uncle has a little stock off cattle & a little farm. He told me if I would settle in this countrie he would help me all he could. I know this is a healthy countrie & that is a great thing.

Well, I will change my subject. I am glad to know the ring suited so well. You wanted to know if I was a musician. No but I am very fond of music. I am glad to know you won the present & injoyed you self so well.

Miss Ella, I must say I have injoyed our little correspondence better than any one I ever held with any person. You ask me not to think hard off you for not answern my quston. I thin[k] more off you for not doing so. Yes, I am really sorry I was so hasty in proposing. You sed you was willing to drop that part off the subject, If I thought it would be best. I diddent meant to drop the subject intireley. I only ment we wouldent go any father with it than we have already went, until we saw each other. I think you air very good & kind to leave it to me to deside.

I am going to make you one more promis & I will fill it as shure as we boath live until that time. I am coming to see you some time between now & next spring. I may come in the early part off the winter & I may not come until the latter part. Please don't think I am tilling you a storie this time. Though you have wright to think that way for I have already told you so many a bout coming.

You sed you thought probly they was some one else a head, No indeed. I only hope you think as much off me as I do off you. By discription & reputation, as you sed in your letter, we might suit each other when we meet & get better acquainted. Though we may not. One might be suited & the other might not.

They is two young Ladies in this countrie I go to see when get the chance though that is very seldom. They air nice young Ladies & one off them air very livly, boath off them aire very good looking.

I am in the store trying to write & they is so much music & racket going on I can hardly write though I like music splendid. As it is getting very late at neight I will close until morning & I have a bout three miles to wride to neight. So will now go & sadle my horse & start. Good Neight.

Sep 3 1888

I will try & finish this letter this morning. This is a beautiful morning, evry thing looks lovly & seames to be livly & pleasant.

I am sorrow to know you are wearried so evry day, though I am glad to know you rest so well at neight. I wish I was thaire to joine your class this morning though the class I will half to joine from now on until a bout Christmas will be with the cows. I will start on faul works this earning to be gone several days though I have no ida when I will be at this Ranch a gan. The Matdor Ranch will be my head quarters this faul.

I know you air tired off trying to read this badly written & composed letter. Mr. Merriman left hear a about the 18th of last month. I was in the Matdor range on a hunt when he left. I hope you have met him by this time. For I know he would like to see youal for he always spoke so well off youal & seam to think a great deal off you & Miss Maggie.

I will change my subject a gan. I hope you will think off me as your best & truest friend. I often think off you & think you air the best young ladie in the world.

Miss Ella, please alow me to say to you in plain words so you may know my intention when I come to see you. If we suit each other I shure mean business at once. If I am talking to plain please for give me. For I think I aught to let you know my intentions. If we please each other, I will promis you that I will treat you well & make you as good living as I can. As I have always told you I am not a wealthy man by any means. [Though] I hope I will always have plenty to eat & waire & pleanty off good friends.

I also intend to have a litter home & live at home before many more years. I mean that is my intention. Weather I will then or not for cirtain I cant say.

Give Miss Maggie my regards & tell hir I hope we all will live to see each other & I hope the time isent far off. If you see Mr. M give him my regards. I will close for this time hoping to hear from youal a gan soon. Your tru & faithful friend until death.

D.C. Kieth.

Good by.

P.S. Direct your letter to Matador Ranch, Motley Co., Texas.

Nov. 2, 1888

(Postmark: Fort Spunky, Tex., notepaper was embossed with a wreathe with the word "Laurel," a logo used in *The Train to Estelline* by Jane Roberts Wood)

To D.C. Kieth
Matador Ranch
Motley (torn) Texas

From: Ft. Spunky, Tex.
Oct. 21 1888

To: D.C. Kieth: Matador Ranch

Your kind and welcome missive was gladly received & read with care. I would have answered it sooner but circumstances was so I could not. I know your forgiving Spirit & kind heart will excuse my tardiness when I give my excuses. Though I don't approve of a letter full of appoliges.

My time have been prencily consumed in teaching & the detestable old cotton patch. I have lost [only] two days & a half in four weeks from picking cotton. Therefore, I only [have] night to wright in & then my hands are too sore & tired to hold the pen. But to-day is a gloomy rainy Sunday. Please excuse my letter if it is so.

I have picked over 25 hundred pounds of cotton this fall. I picked 107 lbs. by noon one day. Pa says he intends to plant a big crop of cotton next year. I intend to claime acres enough to make one bale of cotton & then I can go to the "Fair." My sister & brother-inlaw are going to the Fair this week, And poor me, will have to stay at home & pick cotton.

I don't mind hard work when I enjoy good health. "I don't look to be as stout as I realy am." All of our family have been sick with the chill & fever, accept sister Maggie & myself. Though it may be our time next, for we have just got through eating and shivering over a fine water-melon, which Pa cut & Ma scoled all the time we was eating it.

It is still raining & have been for the past 8 hours. We will have a few days rest from the field, but it will be the sewing ma-chine's turn next. I trust we will get through with our hardest work by Xmas & then I expect I will have to be house keeper, as si[s]-ter Maggie's school will commence in Nov. & Carrie my youngest sister will be in school all winter. But, if I can leave home I may go to school at "Eulogy Bosquey Co." about six mont. I cant hardly give up the idea to think my happy school days are finished. I will teach a writing class at Ft Spunky when the crops are all gathered. I am very much out of practice now.

You spoke of leaving but didn't say whare you was going. I am glad you went to see your relatives before you took your departure & listened to their advise. O how fortunate we all should derm our selves, to have one whom we can confide in & receive instruc-tions from. Rest assured that I will forgive you for being frank in expressing your thoughts & intentions. I often think & almost feel ashamed of [how] pl[ain] I have been writing to a compara-tive strangger. Please excuse my simplicity. I have told you in my former letters, if we ever met, you would find me to be a rustic girl.

I think I have many warm friends, though friends faces prove to be foes some times. I highly appreciate the compliments you have bestowed on me. I dare say I am worthy of them. I am delited to know that our correspondence have been a pleasure to you, it was an agreeable surprise to me indeed. I feel highly complimented to know that my letters are regarded worthy of an answer. I almost hesitate to answer your letters sometimes, for fear I cannot write as good one as I received. I can only return your compliments by appreciatting your letters & the little gift that you sent me. A good correspondent should be valued very highly by evry one. It tis with me at least.

Mr. Merriman is in the country. I havent had the pleasure of meeting him, if he returns without calling to us I will be very angry with him.

I forgot to tell you in my last letter about meeting one of my old sweethearts "at the Association," whom I hav'nt saw nor scarsley heard from in six years. He was'nt near so good looking as he was when I saw him last. I told him I believe his girl had gone back on him if he had any. He said he did'nt have any & would soon be on the old bachleors list & then be dispised by all the fair maids. I gave him the pretiest young ladie of our neighbor-hood for a sweetheart. Which was the best I could do for him.

We have'nt so many intertainments this fall as we had last. Some bad boys broke up our spelling match. But have prayer meeting instead. The rain has seaset & a norther is blowing. I don't recond it mades any difference, for there isn'nt any one out, but the cotton pickers & the cowboys, excuse my jokes please. We [have] a great deel of sickness through out the country. One death last week, an infant.

We have all made very good crops this year. We may enjoy some nice parched gubers [sweet potatoes] when you com if you like them. I will close for fear I will intrude upon your time trying [to] read this & as I have some three or four other letters to write [before] mail day.

Deep in the well springs of the memory, may a rich pearl of good wishes rest dedicated for your true & faraway friend.

Ella Cribbs.

Many good wishes to you in the future. Write soon. E. E. C.

Nov 30, 1888
(Postmark: Fort Spunky Tex)

To: Mr. D.C. Kieth
Matador Ranch
Motley Co. Tex

From: Ft. Spunky Tex
Nov 29 1888

To D.C. Kieth

Kind & absent friend, I will endeavor to answer your welcome of a recent date. I had begun to think you wan't going to write to me any more. I promply answered yours of "Aug." I am sorry you din't get it. I am afaried I cant write a very interesting one tonight, as I am very tired & sleepy. I hav'nt hardly had time to get a good breath since I came home.

The farmers will soon be through gathering their crops, potatoes crops yield better this year than common. We made 150 bu. on three-fourth acres. In facat evry thing in the vegtable line done well this year. I have picked about 6000 lbs. cotton this fall. 191 lbs was my best days picking. We are through with our cotton, but sister Carrie & I have a bale ingaged to pick. I hope we will get through before "Xmas" as we anticipate having a "Xmas tree" & a lively time in general, not withstanding the times "& if the 'lord is willing."

And if we all get well. Brother Dan is very sick at present with fever. Chills & fever are quite numerous in this vicinity. I am almost sick to-night. Maggie & I went visiting yesterday & got very cold riding on the parrie & attended a storm partie the night before at our brother-inlaws. "He" gave us a nice pound partie the 8th instant. He said he would give us a well leap-year partie New Years. We might, so all of us girls may have a fair showing, & all the atvantge of the only year given to the girls.

You wanted to know if I was tired [of] writing or married. I have not done either. I am afraid I will be left till next leap year, as I have failed to address any of the young gentleman on the subject of matrimony, though I have been contemplating matrimony for some time. Though I don't think I will ever get any farther than thoughts. I know I can do my share of thinking. It may be my fate to lead a life of single-bless [or] wretchedness. I would rather live & die an old maid than to get a mean man for a husband, or lead an unpleasant life like some people I know of.

I think Mr. Merriman have treated us real bad. He hav't come to see us yet. I understand he is keeping the beaf market in Granbury. As you are going to farming & can't come this winter, be sure & come next summer as that is the time the farmers & cut-terflies play & sing.

I would like if you could be with us Xmas. I expect to start to school after New Years. I did think I would spend Xmas near Ft. Worthy but will not get off.

Excuse this note & all mistakes especially writing for I sprained my right arm very badly, carrying and packing heavy cotton sacks. Many good wishes to you in your rough life of cow driving. And may happiness & success crown you through life is the wish of your little friend.

Ella___

Dec 8, 1888

(Postmark: Matador Tex)

To: Miss Ella Cribbs
F. T. Spunkey,
Hood Co. Texas

EMPTY ENVELOPE

Jan 22, 1889

(Postmark: [Teepee City?] Tex.)

To: Miss Ella Cribbs,
F. T. Spunky
Hood Co. Texas

From: Teepee City
Motley Co. Texas.
Jan 21 1889

To: Miss Ella Cribbs

Kind & tru friend. I am happy to know I have the opportunity off answern you once more. Your kind & most welcom letter reach me the 16th & I was so glad to hear from [you] & hear you had such a nice Xmas. I was all alone Xmas week, So you can imagine what a livly time I had. They is a young man camped with me. Though they taken him a way Xmas to help drive a hird off beaf cattle to Childress. We had a very good snow out hear sevral days ago. Though we aire having fine weather now.

The parties you spoke off in your last letter [Leap Year pound parties] that [isn't] to live in this countrie. I new off them but wasent acquainted with them. Yes, I was once [on] a cow hunt with Mr Dupree a bout six years ago, but don't expect would know him now as I haven't seean him since.

I will change the subject. I expect I will work on the trail this year as I think I can get more for my work thair than I can on the ranch. This outfit I think will drive a hird up to the Nation or to Colorado or Montania. I don't think they know yet them selvs just whaire they will drive & as I don't know weather I will be hear next summer or not.

I will come down to see you in March if it is agreeable. Now I will not disseave you this time. Will shure come if nothing hapons more than I am expecting. When I hear from you a gan I can tell you what day to look for me. Though you spoke in your letter off Nor off going to school a bout six month this winter & spring. Probly you will not be at home in March. If not I can prospond coming until next faul. I think the present you sent is very nice indeed. I appreciate them very much & I am glad to know you aire so well pleased with the present I sent to you.

I am also glad to know you have appreciated our correspondent so well. I can return the compliments. I never had a correspondent in my life I injoyed any more than I have ours. I am glad to know the past year past away so I with you. So it did wth me in regard to our corrosponden[ce]. So I hope this year will be as pleasant or pleasenter than the past. I hope you dident get offended at me for speaking about you working in the field. I am shure I dident mean to hirt you fealins by any means. I have worked a many day in the field with my sister when I was a very small boy. Though she was a bout grown. As you sed a bout you self, she dident work in the field because she like to. It was because we was poor & she was wiling to help all she could. Though as I sed in my last letter I think you air so kind to tell me all those things. You ask me to not blame you for not ansern my question in the last letter. Cirtinly I don't. I think you air wright by not doing so & I am ashamed off my self for asking so much off you before we saw each other. When I come you will find me to be a very plain man & not very livly. Though I think I could injoy my self talking with you very much.

How far is it from Granbery to Ft. Spunky. I suppose that is the place I will get off the train. I will stop at Ft. Worth one day & will drop you a note from thaire so you will know for cirtain what day to look for me.

Well, I will bring my badley written letter to a close asking you to excuse blotches & mispelts words. I send my best wishes to youal. Write soon to your tru friend.

D.C. Kieth

Mar 23, 1889

(Postmark: [Ben]jamin, Tex., embossed clutched fist on the envelope)

To: Miss Ella Cribbs
F. T. Spunkey
Hood Co. Texas

Benjamin
Knox Co Texas
March 20 1889

To: Miss Ella Cribbs

Far a way friend. I take the gratest off pleasure this lovly eav. in writing you a few lines. Please excuse me for writing a gan so soon. I am at this time in Knox Co. at my uncles. Him & I will go to Benjamin to morrow. I have ben plowing to day for the first time in a bout six years. He has a very prity farm. We planted some corn this morning. I layed out the corn ground & he droped it & covered it.

I landed hear day before yesterday & my uncle & I wrode over a gradeal off the countrie yesterday & I selected a peas off school land for a home. So that will be our business at Benjamin to fix up the papers concerning the land. Now I think I am telling you what I have to try to make you think I am wealthy, for I own but little. Though I hope I may own more in the further days. I am trying now to get me a little home so I may be able to settle down some day & make my own living & be my own boss. I made my own living as it is but cant be my own boss all to gether. My uncle has two children, a son & daughter. They air boath grown.

I don't get lonsome hear like I did in that old camp on Peas River near TeePee City. I hope I will never half to stay in another cow camp, but I may be glad to get to stay in one next winter. Though I think not if I keep my health & right mind. I expect to be at the Matador Ranch the first off April to comens work a gan. So I hope I may find a letter thaire from you when I return. We air having fine weather at this time & the grass is growing very fast.

Well, as I cant think off any thing to write that would interest you. I will bring this badley written & composed letter to a close. I send my regards to Miss Maggie & ask you to except off my best love. I remain your tru friend as ever.

D.C. Kieth

Good earning.

April 12, 1889
(Postmark: Fort Spunky, Tex.)

To. Mr. D.C. Keith [sic]
Matador Ranch
Motley Co./ Texas

From: Ft. Spunky Tex
Apr 8 1889

To: Mr. D.C. Kieth

Absent but true friend. It tis with pleasure I [take] this pleas-ant opportunity to reply to your two last welcome missives which I perused with much care and interest.

I was glad to know you was well & doing well. But how can you to limit your stay in the noted cow camps. Two more of our yong men left for the west to follow the same occupation last Wednesday. I dont know what we will do if a few more of the boys leave the neighbor-hood. As they are generaly the life of the country or a house-hold. But we have enough left to run the Sunday school & spelling match.

I had lots of fun last Sat. night. All the girls from our side of the neighbor-hood had the pleasure of an escort home but poor me. Two of the girls was about 15 years old & one of the boys is about 16, a school mate, & might say all children. I told them they needn't think I was going to walk by my self & let the bugers catch me. We all had a good laugh & Sister Carrie's escort told me I could ride his horse. I ask him if it was gentle, he said no, But I could brake it. I thanked him & told him I didn't wish to be the first lady to ride it, especially at night. Though when we started all three of the boys called brother Dan to ride their horses. I finally rode one horse with Dan to keep from teasing the children to much.

Well, I have my hands full at present. Sister Maggie has gone to Thorp Springs (about 20 miles north of us on the river) to school. Her intention is to finish her education for a yr. I expect she will attend the summer Normal, if she does she will be absent the grater part of the year.

The Sun. school have elected me to fill her vacancy. I am now teacher & secetary both of Sun. school & spelling, besides correspon-dence, but seems like more one does, the more they will have to do. I don't think we ought to complain of our duty. May school will be out the last of this month. Then the field will be my daily companion in labor, I dare say. Wether it will be in my mind or not. The farmers are all through plainting corn & it is coming up nicely.

Mr. Merriman havnt made his aperance yet, though I have been informed he is still in Granbury. Oh! I liked to forgot to tell you about the wedding we had in Ft. Spunky, last the 28th. Our piretiest damsel has forsaken single-blessedness to share the future with a nice young man of her choice.

As I have no more news of interest I will close as it is growing late & I have to rise earley. Write soon to your true friend. Many good wishers to you in your new home.

Ella Cribbs.

April 24, 1889
(Postmark: Jayton, Tex.)

To: Miss Ella Cribbs.
F.T.Spunkey
Hood Co. Texas

From: Jayton PO
Kent Co. Texas
April 18 1889

To: Miss Ella Cribbs

Absent but kind friend. I take my pencil in hand this bright & beautifull eave. to try to pass off the lonsom moments in writing you a few lines. It has ben so long since I received a letter from you.

Though I am satisfied they is a letter at the ranch at this time for me from you. But I hardly think I will have any chance to get my mail from the ranch before June or July. The last letter I received from you was a bout the 15th or 20th off Febuary last.

I written to you a bout the 10th or 12th off March from my old Peas River camp & also written a gan the 20th from Benjamin. Though I know not weather you received eather off my letters or not, but I hope you did & do trust they found you well & injoying your self. I am well at this time & hope thease few lines will find youal well.

I am in Kent Co. at the time near Jayton PO awaiting for the general works to comens on Double Mountains wich will comens the lst off May. I am still working for the Matador Company. I left the ranch the 3rd day off the month. Mr. J.C. is camped a bout 15 miles west off this place, though I haven't sean him for some time but expect will see him in a few days. I have sean seveal off my good old friends since I left camps. I like so much to meet them & talk over old times.

This is a beautifull countrie now. The grass is growing fast & evry thing look lovly. I believe I written to you in my letter off January I was thinking of going up the trail this year. They give me my choice to cow hunt or go up the trail. So I thought I had rather cow hunt.

Has Mr. M. evr ben to see youal yet. I received a letter from him some time ago & he sed he hadent sean you since he went down but was going to see you in a few days. I think so much off him for I think he is such a nice & Kind young man.

Well, I will half to bring my letter to a close for this time. Give my regards to Miss Maggie. I do hope when I return to the ranch, I will find a long letter from you with good news in it. I am your tru & faithful friend.

D. C Kieth

Good by.

Oct 4, 1889
(Postmark: For[t Sp]unky Tex)

To: Mr. D.C. Kieth
Matador Ranch
Motley Co. Texas

From: Ft. Spunky Texas.
Sep 29 1889

To: Mr. D.C. Kieth:

Kind and far-away friend. I will attempt to answer your welcome letter this dreary & drisley Sun-day. We were going to singing this morning, but it rained.

Cotton picking I believe is the order of the day. We "the farmers" are quite busy reaping our yearly harvest. The Aug. drouth injured the cotton considerably. I have only picked 28.74 lbs. I made ten dollars & thirty-five sents, picking for others before ours opened.

We have a cold wind from the north all last week & bad colds is the result of there-fore. I am very much disappointed in not having you to visit us this winter. But come if the opportunity affords and rest assured, your visit will be appreciated & a welcome by us all.

I would like so much to form your acquaintance, personaly. I always enjoy & esteem your letters. Many thanks for the compliments & esteem which you have bestowed up on me. I will return the same honors which is due you for yours. You can't appreciate my letters any more than I do yours & the gifts which you have presented to me. If or when we close our correspondence shall I send your letters, photo & ring back? I know it is the custom to exchange letters when a correspondence close of this kind. But if you havnt burnt mine, you may do so when we quit writing. Though it is agreeable with me for our correspondence to continue, as long as we remain single, or as long as you wish to write.

You spoke about marrying. I may be mistaken, but I think it is right to marrie when people can suit them selves & get their true companions. Though I have almost disided to be an old maid. If I live to see the 27th of next Oct. I will be 25 years old, though I don't feel like I was out of my teens. It is true I have admires & opportunities to marrie but_____. If I ever marrie I want to get my equal in evry respect & get a good husband & made a good wife & live & made happy in evry respect. Then our home would be heaven on earth. As I have so often heard the above expression used.

You must excuse my frankness and simplicity, and especially my inquisitiveness about your people. As I have told you before I am a very plain spoken girl. I expect too much so, for my own good. Mr. James Kieth is the city mars[h]el of Cleburne. His brother Will was his deputy last year.

Sister Maggie has gone back to Thorp's Spring to attend school this year. I miss her so much. If nothing prevents she will be gone 8 months. Perhaps I will attend school at Ft. Spunky this winter, as Pa has just told us our former & favorite teacher has been employed to teach our winter term.

I will close for fear I will wearry your patients in trying to read this badly written & composed letter. Write soon & a long letter to your true & faraway friend.

Ella Cribbs.

[Dec] 4, 18[89]
(Postmark: Della Plain, Tex.)

To: Miss Ella Cribbs
F.T. Spunkey
Hood Co. Texas

From: Della Plains
Cloid [Floyd] Co., Texas
Nov 30 1889

To: Miss Ella Cribbs

My absent friend. I take my pencil in hand once more to try & write you a few lines in ansern to your kind & most welcom letter off Sep 29th wich I received Several days since. I am almost ashame to write as I have ben so long about anser you. Will you please for give me this time for I have ben very study [steady] at work all faul & I am still very buizy. I came in from my last cow hunt the 19th & came out hear the 25th & will probly be hear 7 or 8 days yet. I & 5 other men at this time is out on the plains near Della

Plains birning fire gards a round the Matador beaf pasture. We have a bout sixty miles to birn & I will be very glad when we get don for it gets very cool up hear some times. The last cool spell they had out hear, they was 4 or 5 cow boys & two freighters froze to death near the line of [New] Mexico. I ust to think I would like to live on the plains, but I don't think I will ever live on them any longer than I can help. Though the land is very fine & will rais most any thing, so the people say that livs out hear. But I do not expect to make a living altogether farming, though I would like to have a little home off my own so as to rais such as I neaded for my own use.

Well, I will write on some other subject for a while. You wanted to know what to do with my picture & ring I gave you. I am willing for you to keep them if you lik & I would be very glad to keep your photo if we should ever stop our correspondence. Though I will be very glad to keep it up as long as we are single, for I like so much to read a letter from you. Donnot think because I haven't written to you for so long I had forgotten you, for I had not. I don't think a day ever pases but what I think off you. I often think I would like so much to get pirsonely acquainted with you as we have ben writing to each other so long & seame to be so well pleased on bouth sids so far as we know off each other. As you sed in your last letter I believe every pirson ought to mairrie if they can get thaire tru companion.

Miss Ella, I think a gradeal of you & also think you would make any man a good & tru wife. I only hope when I mairrie if I ever, that I will get as good women for a wife as I think you would be.

Well, I will make you one more promis & will full fill it if it is in my power to do so, provided it is agreeable with you. I gess I will stay out hear this winter & I will come to see you next spring if agreeable. Though I want you to set the time for me to come & I will sure come if nothing hapons more than I am expecting & if we donot suit each other we can still be good friends as ever. If we do suit, my intentions will be to bring you back with me, provided you will come. Please excuse me for talking so plain as we air straingers, though you do not seam much like a strainger to me. You seam more like some one I new always.

If we suit each other I will have a home for you & will promis to treat you well & make the best living I can. I am a free man & will half to settle down & build up as I can, but I think I have enough to make a good living. If I don't hapon to two much bad luck, off corse we all have that risk to run.

I think you must be a good cotton picker. I never picked cotton a day in my life. So I expect you could beat me verry bad. Though I was raised on a farm, my uncle that rais me dident rais any cotton.

Give my regards to Miss Maggie. I will bring my letter to a close for this time hoping it will find youal well. I remain you tru friend as ever.

D.C. Kieth

P.S. I direct your letter as last one, I mean as the one you written last. Good Neight. D.

Jan 30, 1890

(Postmark: Matador, Tex., one page only, writing on front and back)

To: Miss Ella Cribbs
F.T. Spunky
Hood Co. Texas

From Teepee City, Texas
Jan 25 1890
To: Miss Ella Cribbs

Absent friend your welcome letter off Jan 12th reach me the 19th. I was very glad to hear from you though was sorrow to hear off your mother being sick. I hope this letter will find youall well. I am well & injoying my self splendly considering evry thing. I injoyed my self splendid Xmas day. I taken Xmas dinner with one off my neighbor friends, a family by the name off Wells. We had plenty off egg nog & a fine diner. I was at that time camped 3 miles on the river below Mr Welles. I am bourding with him now feeding some beaf cattle for the company I am working for. I think they aim to ship them for early market wich will be some time in April. We live on a river know as Tung [Tongue] River. My Aunt that I have spoken off to you in my former letters died last Tuesday morning was a week ago. I got the news that she was very sick & went to see hir, but I was to late. She was ded & bearied when I got thaire. I thought so much off hir for she was cirtainly as a mother to me. My uncle livs a bout 40 miles south off this place. He has two children, a Son & Daughter. They air a bout grown, his son mairred . . .

Mar 3, 1890
(Postmark: Fort Spunky, Tex.)

To: Mr. D.C. Keith [sic]
Teepee City
Motley Co Texas.

From: Ft. Spunky Tex.
Mar 2 1890

To: Mr. D.C. Kieth

Kind and esteemt [esteemed] friend; Your letter came to han[d]
in due time. I recond you are very much vexed and have gone back
on me, but I can'nt help it. I am confident your kind heart will
forgive my tardins this time—when I tell you I have been very sick
with La grippe since I received your letter. But am quite well at
present—I would have ans. you by last Fri. mail—but 'twas so cold
it kept me buisy turning round by the fire to keep from freezing. "La
grippe" is an epidemic going through the country & is very fatal
when followed by pneumonia. Only 8 students (of one school in
"Johnson" Co.) died in one week with it.

I am sorry indeed to hear of your anties death—secialy as she
was so dear to you—for a mother I think ought to be prized above
all others. I haint had the trial looseing mine and some times I
don't think I could bear to give her up in death. Though—we ca'nt
live togather here on earth always, so to speak; but we can beyond
this vale of tears. Ma is getting well but very slow. The Dr dismiss
into her case the last time he came.

I am delighted to know you are well & enjoying your-self so
well & that you have a family to board with. I gudge [judge]
that is a treat compared with camping. I am also glad you had a

nice Xmas for that is more than I can say. Mine was nice enough but I was too tired to enjoy my self much. We did'nt pick cotton Christmas day—but I worked hard all the same. I spent the fore noon in cooking dinner, & my dinner was highly complimented by all that dined with us. And in the afternoon I got my (memorandum) book & counted up earnings & expences of the year.

I made $45.60cts out side of home & spent $10 for my self & spent the remainder on the family. Besides I made a full hand at home. I picked cotton 4 months to a day & only lost 2 weeks out of the 4 months. I don't intend to work so hard this year (i.e.) if I can help myself & I think I can. I am chief house keeper at present as the girls is in school.

Please excuse me til I go & cook dinner—it is now 12 o'clock but 'tis Sun & I don't recond it will make any difference if dinner is late. Well; I have finished dinner & fixed my-self trying to finish your letter. The young people sent me word to meet them at the school-house, this we to assist them organize a singing class but 'tis too cold to leave the fire for such a little purpose. I am afarid the neighbor-hood is too dead to survive.

I am sory you misconstrued a potion of my letter—but of course I am willing to abid by your decision, also will be willing to close the correspondence when it suits you. I can say it has been very pleasant to me & feel complimented you have enjoyed & esteemed my letters as well as you say you have. Yes, I trust our friend-Ship will always be endless as the ring that is on my finger for which I am wareing it for. You can imagine how much I prize the tokens you was so kind to present me. Shall we exchange our letters or not? Write soon to your faraway & tru friend.

Ella Cribbs.

"*Do not hasten to bid me adiu*
But remember the heart you are breaking
And the girl who l_____s you so tru."

Mar 18, 1890
(Postmark: Teepee City, Tex.)

[Ella's writing in ink at bottom of his letter: "Mr. D.C. Keith [*sic*]
Matador Ranch Motley Co. Tex."]

To: Miss Ella Cribbs.
F. T. Spunky
Hood Co. Texas.

From: TeePee City, Texas
March 16 1890

To: Miss Ella Cribbs

My kind friend. I take the greatest off pleasure this bright &
beautiful morning in trying to answer your kind & most arlier letter.
I received several days since. Cirtainly I will forgive you for not
writing sooner. I was so sorrow to hear you had ben sick & was glad
to know you had gotten well. I am well at present & have had good
health all winter & I am glad I can say that much for my self. For
I do think good health is the best thing on earth. I have ben blessed
with good health the most off my life. I will change my subject.

This countrie is began to look very pirty once more as the grass
& weeds is coming fast & the little flowers air began to show their

appearance over the beautiful prairies. Grass is arlier in this part off the countrie this spring than last. We will go to gather a hurd off cattle a bout the 20ᵗʰ to drive to Kansas. I will work on the trail this year more for a change off work than any thing else. At the same time, I know trail work is the hardest work in the cow business.

I will change my subject again. So far stoping our correspondence I do not wish to stop, as long as you air so kind to answer my letter as you have always ben. For I do have grate respect for you & appreciate your kind letters very much. I am sorrow I misunderstood a part off your last letter. I hope you will forgive me & let us be good friends as we have always ben. Though if we should quit writing you will please birn my leters if you have any off them & I will do what ever you wish me to do with yours. I have all off your letters in my trunk I believe except 2, that is one lying on the table I am writing on & I carried one in my pocket on a cow hunt until it was very near worn out. So I birnt it as I was afraid I would lose it before I returned to the ranch. I will bring my poly written & composed letter to a close. **You will please direct your next letter to Matador Ranch Texas.** I send my regards to all. I trus you will write soon & a long letter to your tru friend as ever.

D.C. Kieth.

On an additional page included with the above letter,
D.C. writes in brown ink:

You tell me your heart I am breaking. Do not think that I never regret. That for me a fond heart has ben aching or that you I can ever forget. Adieu all not hasten to bid you my heart shall be ever thine own, though miles from my sight may have hid you. I still love my darling alone.

At the bottom of his last page, Ella later notes in pencil:

> You Tell me your heart I'm breaking
> Do not think that I never regret
> That for me a fond heart has been aching
> Or that you I ever can forget
> Adieu I'll not hasten to bid you my heart
> It shall be ever thine own
> Though miles from my sight may have hid you
> I still love my darling alone.

Apr 18, 1890

(Postmark: Fort Spunky, Tex., pressed baby rose in letter)

To: Mr. D.C. Kieth
Matador Ranch.
Motley Co. Tex

From: Ft. Spunky Texas
Apr 16 1890

To: Mr. D.C. Kieth:

Faraway and kind friend; After the elapse of several days I'll try & answer your most kind and welcome missive. I was glad to know you were well. Yes, I do agree with you, I know good health ought to be prized above all rules.

Well, I have been having the chills since I wrote to you last, though [I] have them broke and feel quite well at present. These were the first chills I've had since '80. As you say I generally have good health & enjoy it. I am incline to think this country is getting sickly & have been beging Pa to go father [farther] west i.e. south west.

In-fact he has concluded to go down in "Tom Green" Co. next summer on a prospecting tour. "Mr Thompson" my brother-inlaw is speaking about going to your part of the country to buy land. They moved near Ft. Worth last Dec. where the land is better than this, as he is a cotton farmer. Oh! I tried so hard to go to see them in this month, but failed to get off as work time over took me. The farmers have a fine prospect for a good crop at present, but we ca'nt count on anything being made till it is gathered.

Oh! You ought to see my garden, it is the finest one in the country; we haveing greens for two weeks. I call it mine because I have planted & worked it. As it rained today & the horses are rested Pa says he will send me in the pasture in the morning to look for some cows. Do'nt you know I'll have a fine time for I do enjoy horse back riding; & we have a splendid saddle horse & a good saddle.

Oh! I went to church twice last Sun. for the first time since last Aug. I tell the people we all might as well be living on the frontiers as far as the preaching is conserned. But we will have preaching here on each second Sun. from now on.

I do enjoy good preaching better than any one I recond. The Methodst will have preaching next Sun. & dinner on the ground, on "Georgia's Creek." Come down & we will go over, 'tis only 5 miles over there.

Well, I recond that is as much as you want to read about that subject. I'll change it however. We attended a nice partie a few weeks a go & started to another last week, but the waggon tire run off & we had to walk one mile back home. I do'nt dance but enjoy my self teasing those I'm well acquainted with.

Sister Maggie is coming home in a few weeks from school & I will be so glad. You may burn my letter as you requested me to do yours. (I have all yours yet & enjoy reading them over.) I do'nt expect they are worth sending back, I mean I recond you are making ready for your journey to "Cansas." I wish you a pleasant trip and lots of fun. How long will it take to drive a herd through?

Please excuse all mistakes and write soon to your far-away friend. As ever

Ella Cribbs.

May 8, 1890
(Postmark: Teepee City, Tex.)

To: Miss Ella Cribbs.
F. T. Spunky
Hood Co. Texas.

From: Teepee City, Texas
May 5 1890

To: Miss Ella Cribbs

Absent friend. I take my pencil in hand to try & answer your kind & most welcome letter wich I recieved several days since & was certainly glad to hear from you once more. I trust you will forgive me for not writing sooner for I have ben so buisy I have hardly had time to write to any one. I was glad to learn you had got the chills broke. I hope this letter will find youal well. I also trust youal air well at this time.

I just returned from the rail road. We drove our hurd to Giles, Texas & shipted from thair.[77] That is about 50 or 60 miles north off this place. I think we will ship the balance off cattle from Childress. I hope so any way for very near evry hurd this out fit has drove to Giles, they has ben a man very badly hurt or killed. It seames to be an unluckey place. One of our men got killed on this trip. His horse fell with him & he never did speake any more. He lived about 45 hours. His name was James Carder. He had ben working for this company a bout 5 or 6 years off & on.[78]

Well, I will change my subject. We air now camped near Teepee City awaiting for fa[r]ther orders. I think our next work will be to gether another hurd & drive out on the plains to the beaf pasture. Though I don't know, I just gessing at what I think is to be done. I think we will comens shiping beaf cattle some time in July & then we will be shiping the most off the summer & faul. I believe we air going to have the finest grass in this countrie this year than has ben for several [years]. I believe they has already more rain fell this spring than fell before in the spring in 6 or 7 years. The wheat & oats on the Matador farmes looks very fine. The land in this countrie seames to be better for small grane [grain] than any

---

77. Giles was located in Donley County at the Fort Worth & Denver Railway stock pens where cattle were held nearby during trail-driving days and then loaded on rail cars.

78. The Matador Ranch Cowboy List/Cowboy Roster noted N.J. Carter with a start date May 1884. Southwest Collection, Texas Tech Library, j:/public/records/mat-list.doc, accessed 1994/08/01.

other kind. They is plenty off school lands in this countrie a pirson can buy for two dollars per acre & get 30 years to pay for it in.

I will half to close for this time. Please excuse pencil & poor writing & spelling. I send my good wishes to youal. Hoping I may hear from you a gan soon, your friend.

D.C. Kieth

Good Earning.

July 1890

(Postmark and date obscured: Matador [Tex], notepaper embossed with capitol buildings)

To: Miss Ella Cribbs.
F. T. Spunkey,
Hood Co. Texas

From: Matador Ranch
Motley Co. Texas
July 27 1890

To Miss Ella Cribbs

Absent friend. I take grate pleasure this breight & beautifull Sabath morning in trying to write you a few lines in answer to your kind & most welcom letter I received the 16th off this mounth & was certainly glad to hear from you once more. The cause off me not getting your letter any sooner, I was not at the ranch.

I just returned the 16th from a cow hunt. My cow hunting is over with untill faul, that is untill the 1st off Sept. I am at this time working for my self on my section of land, trying to fix me up a little home. I will go to work for the company a gan the 1st off Sept. A man by the name of F. M. Wells & my self taken up a Section off land in the Matador horse pasture. Mr. Wells is the man I boarded with last winter while I was feeding some stears for the company. Our land is 2 miles east off the ranch. We divided the section east & west. I taken the north side & Mr. Well the south side.

The company had dug a well wich they thought was near the line off thair land & my land, but thought it was on thair land. So I had lines run out & the well proved to be on my land wich makes it worth a gradeal more. Mr Campbell the ranch boss sed he was glad that I was so luckey as to get the well & I believe he is, for he is a good man & a good friend of mine. Mr. Campbell is a man off good standing & controles a gradeal off property, but is a poor mans friend.

Well, I will try & change the subject a little. I trust you will for give me for not writing sooner for I have ben buisy evr since I recieved your letter. I also ask you to excuse. It is the best I can do at present. I am at this time out at my litter western home, sitting under a arbor trying to write to you. I will go to the ranch this erning but would not have time to write while I was thair.

I want to go see my sister this summer if I can get my work done in time. I think I can start down by the 10th or 12th next mounth. She livs in Jackbo, a bout half way between Jacksboro & Graham on a creek by the name off Salt Creek.

The young man you spoke off that invited you to his weding I suppose is mairred. Did you attend the weding? I do not wish you or him any harm, but I was glad to hear it was Miss Ella Hudgins in place off Miss Ella Cribbs. If they air mairred & Miss Ella Hudgins is as good woomen as I believe you air, he ought to be a moung the hapies mens on earth. Now don't think I am just writing for pass time. For I mean evry line I have written.

As I have told you in some off my farmer letter I do think you air one amoung the best women on earth. You air the first young Ladie I evr corresponded with that would tell me a bout working out in the feal. The most off young ladies wants a young man to think they do'nt do any hard work. I realy do'nt think the feal is a womens place, but that is one thing maks me think you air so good & kind as to help your father.

My Brother & Sister & my self have worked many a day in the feal to gether in our raising up. We was raised by one off our uncles & he was a poor man & we had to help him while he was raising us. Though he was always good & kind to us. His name was J. G. Brazelton. He is ded now.

Well, I will bring my letter to a close prity soon for the wind is blowing so hard I can hardly write. I know you will get weried out trying to read this scribbled up letter.

If I go to Jackbo this summer I would like very much to come to see you if thair is no objectins. I would like so much to meet with you as we have ben writing to each other so long. I send my regard & good wishes. Write soon & often to your tru friend as evr.

D.C. Kieth

Sep 5, 1890
(Postmark: Fort Spunky, Tex.)

To: Mr. D.C. Kieth
Matador Ranch
Motley Co. Texas

From: Ft. Spunky Texas
Sept 8 1890

To Mr. D.C. Kieth

Esteem friend: I am very sorry indeed I didn't receive your letter in time to have answerd it before you left the ranch for your visit to your sisters. But why didn't you come on down here anyway?

Yes, I would have been delighted to form your personal acquaintance too. I almost know you would have enjoyed your self if you had come. I believe I have spent the most deliteful summer I ever did. I have actively spent this summer going to protracted meetings, picnics, visiting and receiving visitors. We finished hoeing the last wk. in June & the first wk. in July. Bro Dan & I went to see Mrs. Thompson our sister of whom lis 2 mi. east of Ft. Worth in Tarrant Co. I only stayed 10 days & was sick 6 days so you see I never enjoyed my visit much—but they came home with me & stayed 2 weeks.

I trust you had a nice time while at your sisters. Are you just now making the visit to see her which you spoke of long ago? We uster live in Young [County] & "Graham" was our P. O.

Well, we won't get to go west this year as our crop is cut short again. We havn't had a rain since the 6th of June. Corn is very good but cotton is short. Cotton is the staple crop of the farmers here.

I presume you have decided & settled in the glorious west. I think it a wise conclusion, though I don't wish to dictate. A few of our neighbors are selling out & going west. I am very sorry too as they will take off my chum & two of our nicest young gentleman, but I've heard it said the loss of one is the gain of two.

Well—that young man I spoke of marring is still single, (and don't you think he was my escort from singing last Sun. eve.) They have either broke the engagement or have put it off till some indefinite time. He seems to be in a peck of trouble & didn't hesitate to unfold his troubles to me & ask my advise. Of course, I advised him to take her if he could ger her. One of her old sweethearts came this summer on a visit to see som relatives so I am incline to believe he will beat yet. We only have 3 young ladies in this neighborhood named "Ella" and another one went back on her betrothel & it hurt him so he has gone to parts unknown. So that Ella wasn't me either, but she is a friend of mine. I kept her uncle's company before "Sister Carrie" beat me.

Please excuse me for writing so much about us girls & boys. Most all the boys is falling in love with "Carrie" & I expect you would too if you was here, but I beat her getting a resitation for the last day of school. Our school closed last Fri. & I went home with my [favorite] chum & she came home with me on Sat. eve. & stayed till Sun. Her fellow lives at "Ft. Spunky" & of course, he came to see her. Her father don't alow her to keep his company. So you see I [was] helping her too. Don't you think I am a real good girl to help her now when she uster to be my rival, but not with her present admirer.

I am like "Mr. Campbell." I am glad that well is on your land & hope your friend "Mr. Wells" have plenty of water too. For I know something about the inconvenience & scarcity of water in Tex. Pa has just finished a well in our yard. It is about 20 feet deep. I can't hardly keep house without plenty of good water.

Cotton picking, I believe, is the order of the day at present. We commenced Monday which ended our summer's amusements. So, I am helping Pa again which I deem my duty as he is getting old. He was 55 years old last June 17th.

I do indeed appreciate your compliments which you have so frankly past on me, whether I deserve them or not. I believe evry one speaks the same for us girls. I know there is girls whom won't help their fathers, or even mothers, but they are scarce in this country. I am thankful to say we were taught how to do most evry kind of work. As I heard our land lady say once, "The Cribbs girls could do any thing commencing with the blackest pot in the kitchen to the finest fancy work."

I can't say I love to work in the field better than the house like som girls. I do like to pick cotton i.e. when it is better than it is this year. By the crops being short I will not have to work so hard like I did last year. I think I will quit working so hard any way. (So I told our teacher the other day. She said she expect I would [quit] when I died.) For I notice those that don't work spends about as much as those that do work— "But, ah! What does the Bible say?" Well, it just tells us lots of things for us to do & not to do; so I will try to do as I have always tried to do & that is to obey its instructions. Though I don't claim to do right all the time—like many others I get careless.

I will finish some other time as 'tis time to go to the field. I am writing at noon while it is too hot to work.

Sept. 4th. At noon.

I will try to finish my letter today for tomorrow is mail day. Ma is 50 years old today & one of my little nephews is 5 years old. What is your sisters name or rather whom did she marrie? Is "Mr. Wells" your nearest neighbor, or is there many neighbors at all?

What has become of "Mr. Jinkins"? I heard of "Mr. Merriman" this summer. He was at a barbacue at "Glen Rose," the county seat of Sommerville County.

Oh! I must tell you something about my pets; Pa made me a present of a yearling colt & branded it (backwards E or 3) on left shoulder & a friend gave me a little pig one eve while I was there & I brought it home in a flour sack. It [squeals] so at the door evry one threatens to kill it but me & I have to beg for it. I trust this letter will meet you at the Ranch & find you well. Please excuse scribbling & all mistak & write when you can.

As ever your friend

Ella—

Oct 11, 1890

(Postmark: Teepee City.)

To: Miss Ella Cribbs.
F. T. Spunkey
Hood Co. Texas

From: Teepee City
Motley Co. Texas
Oct 10 1890

To: Miss Ella Cribbs

Far a way friend. I take greate pleasure this beautifull faul morning in trying to ansern your most welcome letter I recieved several days since. Cirtainly was glad to hear from you once more, though I had began to think you wasent a going to write any more as you was so long a bout ansern. Yes, I would off like so much to off come down thair last summer though I had no ida off coming unless I hird from you before hand.

You wanted to know is my sister mairried. She [Sophronia] mairried a man by the name of [Henry Taylor] Garner. They mairried in Tenn. We all came from midle Tenn. the faul of '81. They talk off mooving to this countrie if they can sell out in Jack Co. I only hope & trust they will. They dident make hardly any thing in Jack Co. this year. I tried tirble hard to get my Brother inlaw [Garner] to come west with me & look at the countrie when I was down last summer.

I think a man aught to go & look at the countrie wich he is thinking off going to before he moovs his family thair. They is pleanty good lands to be got in this countrie now at two dollars per acre but I don't think it will be long untill it will be taken up by setlers. Home seekers air travling all over the countrie & settling as fast as they can. I have two dollars per acre for my land & would not take fore it. I have several neighbors in sight. Mr. Wells is the clostest. Him & I will be a bout half mile a part. He is a nice man & has a nice famlie.

Well, I will change the subject. I was surprised to hear off that young man you spoke off not beaing mairried, though he is foolish to want hir if she dosent want him. If I evr mairrie I will half to belief the one I mairrie thinks more off me than any one else, weather she does or not. Well, you wanted to know whaire Mr. J. C. was. I think he is still working for the Espuela Land & Cattle Co. I haven't heard from him for some time. Dockum Ranch is his PO office. I have made 2 trips to Kansas City this faul & will start a gan in a few days.

Will close sending regards to all. Write soon to your friend as ever.

D.C. Kieth.

Nov 8, 1890
(Postmark: Fort Spunky Tex)

To D.C. Kieth
Teepee City
Motley Co. Tex.

From: Ft. Spunky Tex
Sun. night, Nov 2 1890

To: Mr. D.C. Kieth

Highly esteemed friend—I recd. your welcome letter several days ago & this is the first opportunity I've had to ans. it. I was glad to hear from you once more—I began to think you had forgot to write. But your letter came which proved you haven't for gotton me. Well, I'm on the tardy roll again. I'm still the same girl I've always been. I didn't forget to write, but like your self, I've been so busy I havn't hardly had time to get a good breath, but if good weather continues, we will soon be through in the field. We only have one bale of scattering cotton to pick yet & the gubers [sweet potatoes] to gather & then the hog-killing & soap-making.

Pa has been very sick the past week & tonight he says he re-conds Carrie & I will have to hall in the corn which he has pulled. I never have harnessed a horse yet, but recond I can learn. There isn't any one to hire. The boys have all gone east to pick cotton. We had church today & had some nice company home with us for dinner.

I'm sorry indeed you didn't come last summer. I'm confident you would have had a nice time, but your letter didn't come in time for me to ans. it before you left the ranch. When may I have the pleasure to look for you again? I trust you had a nice time while at your sisters; also now. Do you think of working in the cattle busi-ness another year? One of our "Johnson Co." friends bid us good bye just 2 weeks ago to night. He has bought in "Dickens Co." or "Motley Co." Perhaps you may meet with him.

Many good wishes for you & write soon to your true friend.

Ella Cribbs.

Mon. night.

I'll write a few more lines tonight. As tomorrow is mail day, though I fear I will not get this to the office as it is election day & Pa can't go. He is some better today. Well, we will not have to do that halling [hauling]. We will swop work with a neighbor. Yes, I can agree with you again in regard to marring. If I ever marry I will have to believe that my betrothd loves me whether he does or not, for I wouldn't appreciate any ones dividd love. But this young lady I spoke of is an exception & is worthy of some nice young man, but I don't think she will ever marry either of those men I spoke of.

As ever   Ella

Nov 20, 1890
(Postmark: Teepee City Tex.)

To: Miss Ella Cribbs
F. T. Spunkey,
Hood Co. Texas.

From: Teepee City,
Motley Co. Texas
Nov 19 1890

To: Miss Ella Cribbs

Kind & true friend. I am happy to know I have the pleasure off ansern you once more. I recieved your kind letter yesterday eav. I have ben gone several days on a trip to Chigago [sic] Ill. I just returned to this place yesturday eav. I am expecting another hurd of cattle at this place this eavning. So, I supose I will half to start to the rail road a gan to morrow with another hurd to ship. I have the contract off shipping for the Matador Company this faul. They pay me thirty dollars per month and board & twenty to thirty extrie for each & evry train off cattle I ship. I have made fifty to sevty dollars per mounth all faul. I think this trip will be my last for this year. You wanted to know if this year would be my last in the cattle buisness. Well, I don't know as I will follow it altogether next year for a living, as I want to try and improve my little home a long as I am able. I am not able to quit work intirly for wages yet, but I do trust they is a day coming when I can & live at home & be my owne boss.

I Have a Sister [Sophronia Kieth Garner] living in Dickens Co. now. She is the Sister I visited last summer in Jack Co. I hadent sean hir before in 5 years. I am better satisfied now than I have ben for years. For I can get to see them now very often. I concider hir my best friend on earth & I know I think as much off hir as a Brother could off a Sister. They have got them a pace off land in a litter settlement by the name of Cottonwood. They air several familys living in that settlement & they have a very good school thair.

You wanted to know when to look for me. I cant say at this time, as I have a gradeal off work laid off to do for my self, provided I don't work for the Company. I have sold my stears & bought horses. I only have a small bunch off horses. I am not able own very many. I am not trying to make you think I am worth very much. I own but little but what little I do own is truly my own.

I would like very much to have a picture off you self in a larger size than the one you sent me & will return it at any time you wish me two. I will close for this sending my good wishes to all. Please write soon to your friend as ever.

D.C. Kieth

Nov 29, 1890
(Postmark: Childress, Tex.)

To: Miss Ella Cribbs.
F. T. Spunkey.
Hood Co. Texas

From: Childress, Texas
Nov 27 1890

To: Miss Ella Cribbs

Absent friend. I take pleasure in writing you a few more lines. This leaves me well & I trust it will find youal well. You spoke in your last letter off your father being sick, I hope he is well at this time. We air holding our cattle in a pastur near Childress at this time, a waiting for cars to ship. Thease cattle will go to Litter Rock Ark, to be fead until spring. The Company sold them to a feader thair by the name of Houston. He wants me to ship them but I gess I will not, as I am anxus to get back to the ranch. They air talking off having a dance at the ranch, as soon as we all get in. So you can gess why I am so anxus to get back. I think this is our last hurd to drive this year. I hope so any way, for it is getting coal to stand neight gard.

Well, I gess Teepee City will be my Post office a gan this winter. I expect I will work for this company another year any way. I don't think I will have very much to do this winter, though I will have a cirtain part off the range to look after & brand large calvs. But I don't think they will be many calvs to brand, as they aire branded up clost. I did aim to work for my self this winter, provided I couldn't made a deal with the company to suit me. So I have made a trade to work for them another year. H.H. Campbell stayed all neight with us the neight before we left the range. He is the ranch manager. He give me a good sendoff a bout my shiping. He sed I was the best shiper that had ever shipped for the Matador Company. Well, I am always glad to know I give satisfaction to [those] I am working for.

You wanted to know when to look for me a gan. I couldn't tell you in my last letter as I dident know at that time, but after the 10th off Dec. I think I can get off for a few days most any time. Now I will leave it with your self what time I may have the pleasure off coming & if I should come, of course. I will let you know what day to look for me & you will be the first I will expect to meet at the dor. For I am a very bashful man, though I believe meeting you would seame more like meeting a friend I new, than a stranger. I will close wishing youal well.

D.C.

Dec 15, 1890
(Postmark: Cleburn Tex., fowarded: Matador, Teepee City: Dec 17 1890)

To: Mr. D.C. Kieth,
Tee Pee City
Motley Co. Texas

From: Ft. Spunky Tex.
Dec 14 1890

To: Mr. D.C. Kieth:

Esteemed friend; Your two last letters was duely recd. & I'll hastly reply to the same tonight as I am going to Cleburne tomorrow. Doubtless you are having a fine this season travling round. I suppose you have had the party you spoke of. How many girls living at the ranch?

Yes, I know you are better satisfied since your sister has moved nearer to you. Have they bought near your land? You ought to have gone to seen your sister sooner as they moved west at once.

Times dosent seem to be so hard with you western folks as 'tis with us farmers. I tell you good forturne makes one feel 100 per sent better any way; it seems as though we never will get ahead any more, besides we all work hard & are very equinomicle [economical].

Well, Xmas is nearly here again. I'm thinking it wil be very dull in the immediate neighborhood. There is talk of having two Xmas trees on the Creek & I have two presents already promised to me, but am afraid I can't return the favor.

If it suits your convenience you may come Xmas wk., but if you can't get off then, most any time will be agreeable with me that suits you. I specified the holidays as that is generally a leisure time with most evry one.

My picture I would send if I had one. I had 6 made last fall but pshaw! They didn't last to get round those that spoke for them before they were finished. But will give one when I can have them taken.

Marriages pshaw! The are just to common to talk about. It seem like evry marriagible person on the "Creek" is marring—only four brides & grooms was at church one Sun. The preachers (I think) have all gone back on "Spunky." We went to church this after noon, but the preacher never did come, so we came back very much disappointed.

I'll close hoping to hear from you soon. Come Xmas if you can.

As ever your true friend

Ella

Dec [_] , [1890]

(Postmark: Childress [Tex])

To: Miss Ella Cribbs
F. T. Spunkey
Hood Co. Tex

Childress. Texas
Dec 21 1890

To: Miss Ella Cribbs.

Absent friend. I take greate pleasure in writing you a few lines to neight. Your letter off Dec 14th reach me a few days a go & was read with pleasure. I am now on my way to F. T. Worth. I landed at this place this earning & will get to F. T. Worth a bout 8 oclock to morrow neight & hope to see you on Xmas day, if nothing presents me from getting thair. Now I trust you will be the first to meet me. I will shur be thair Xmas day if possible.

Will close hoping to see you soon. I am your tru friend as ever

D.C. Kieth

P. S. Goodneight

[Dec 25 1890]

(No postmark or date on envelope)

To: Miss Ella Cribbs
At Home
Ft. Spunkey Tx
Dec 25 1890

Compliments off D.C. Kieth to Miss Ella Cribbs & would like to call & see hir to day. Please mention in your note what time you wish me to come.

(No postmark or date on envelope.)

To: Mr. D.C. Kieth

Present

Compliments of Mr. D.C. Kieth carefuly received & accepted. You may call today about eleven o'clock, this Dec the 25th 1890.

Dec 31, 1890

(Denver & Ft. Worth RR. P.O., office stationary of Deaton, Know
& Co., Wholesale & Retail Grocers, Stone Block, east side of
Swearingen St., Childress, Texas)

To: Miss Ella Cribbs.
F. T. Spunkey,
Hood Co. Texas
Dec 30 1890

To: Miss Ella Cribbs

Absent but tru friend. It is with the gratest off pleasure I write you a few lines to neight. I returned to this place this earning with safty & have alredy met with grate many off my warm friends. [Dean?], Johnie, & I separated at F.T. Worth this morning a bout half past nine oclock, I taken the train for Childress & [May or Mary?] taken the train for [Millsap?]. I believe that was the place they was going, wasent it? Also met two off my cow boy friends at the Fort & we all came up together. They had ben down spending Xmas with relations in Parker & Tarant [Tarrant] Co.

Well, our holidays air over for a while. Next thing is work & I can certainly go to my work with a good & wiling heart. For I can say my Xmas has ben the happies Xmas to me for the past 10 years. As it is getting late I half to close.

Please excuse paper as the PO is closed & this kind was all I could get to neight. Please write at once & let me know if youal returned home saft. I trust you did.

Love & regards to youal. Your tru friend
D.C. Kieth
Good neight.

Jan 24, 1891
(Postmark: Teepee City Tex.)

To: Miss Ella Cribbs
Ft. Spunkey
Hood Co. Tex

From: Teepee City Texas
Jan 23 1891

Miss Ella Cribbs

True Friend. Your kind & most welcom letter reach me the 14th. I [was] glad to know youal had a nice time going home. I trust this letter will find youal well. I am well at this time, though I have ben very sick since I came home.

We have ben having some very rough weather for the past two weeks. A large snow fell near two weeks ago to neight & isent all gone yet & looks as though it might snow a gan before morning.

We have got our winter quarters fixed up right well & we air camped in a countrie whair we have plenty off wood clost to our camp. They air three off us camped to gether. We [have] two horses a peace & have a certain part off the range to look after & brand large calvs. I haven't ben to the ranch since I returned, though I expect I will go a bout the last off this mounth as we have got orders to come in the 31st.

I think they aim to hold a convention of some kind concirning the new town. Motley Co has organised right lately & they is two new towns running for the county seat. The election will come off the 5th off next mounth. It dosent make much difference with me wich town gets the county seat for my land is very near, as close to one as the other.

Seveal off my friends wants me to run for sherrif, but I hardly think I will, for I have got a good and study job. I get thirty dollars per mounth & bourd through the winter & can make from fifty to seventy dollars per mounth through shiping season. I think I can quit working for wages by next faul & comens work for my self.

I am sorrow I diddent stay at Granbury the day I left thair, so we could off had those photos taken. For I could off stayed just as well as not. The cause off me not coming by my uncles was I hird he was in Jack Co. visiting relations.

I recieved a letter from your Brother Dan the day I recieved your letter. He written that Johnie & him self was well.

As it is geting late at neight I will bring my dull letter to a close. Please excuse mispelts words & write soon to your true friend.

D.C. Kieth

Feb 7, 1891

(Postmark: Fort Spunky Tex., forwarded in pencil to Matador, postmark on back: Teepee City, Feb 18 1891)

To: Mr. D.C. Kieth
Matador / Tee Pee City, Tex
From: Ft. Spunky Tex
Feb 6 1991

To: Mr. D.C. Kieth

Most esteemed friend: I recd. [received] your most welcome letter last week & will try to answer it today though I dont feel like I could write much. I was sorry indeed to know you had to get sick after having such a nice time.

Well you are not by yourself being sick—we have all been sick this week, accept Carrie & she was sick last week. Doubtless you will be surprised when I tell you that Dan is at home once more. He only worked two weeks on the brick-yard. As old hands came back they took their former places, so many new ones was left without work. So Dan & another man went to "Galveston" to help find deep water "as he says" & failed to get work there, as that work hadnt begun. Then he came back by "Huston" as he had a friend there—he could have got work there at $40 per month but the small pox was raging so he was afraid to stay.

He has been home 12 days & has been very sick with a cold & light fevers. We are very uneasy about him for he may take the small pox yet. Some of our neighbors wont come near. They say he will have them yet.

Yes, I am sorry too about not staying in town that day. I would have insisted but you seemed to be in a hurry to get back to the ranch, so I wouldnt dictate.

Well, how did you all come out in your meeting yesterday? I suppose you attended. And will you be a canidate for sheriff?

I suppose you enjoy good fires as you are handy to wood & we are having so much disagreeable weather. O we had a fine snow too on the 9th of Jan. It only snowed five hours here, but it rains *evry week, I recond you all have a very nice time as there is three of you all togather. Who is the house-keeper?*

I will close by beging you to excuse all mistakes & penciling for I am writing on my lap by the fire. I trust this will find you well, at least feeling much better than I do.

Write soon to your far away & true friend.

Ella

P. S. Was your horse at "Teepee" for you when you arrived there? E.

Feb 10, 1891
(Postmark: Estacado, Texas)

To: Miss Ella Cribbs
Ft. Spunky
Hood Co. Texas

Office of County and District Clerk, Crosby County,
Attached Counties: Dickens, Lubbock, Motley, Lynn
Sid B. Swink, Clerk

From: Estacado, Texas
Feb 8 1891

To: Miss Ella Cribbs

My true friend. With grate pleasure I write you a few lines this pleasant Sunday eav. Though I haven't any reply from my last letter. But I think they will be a letter at the ranch for me from you when I return. I do trust they will any way. I supose I will get back to the ranch next Wednesday or Thursday.

I landed at this place yesturday eav. Three of us came up to gether in a hack. We came to Floid [Floyd] City the first day & had a dance thair that neight & also had a fine time. So they promised to give us another dance as we came back.

By the way, I went to church to day for the first time since I left Hood Co. It was a Quaker meeting & was the first one I ever was at. Most all those people out hear in this town I believe are Quakers & seam to be very nice & clever.

This is the oldest town I believe in northwest Texas. Our county was attached to this co. though we have a co. seat in our co. now & the name of it is Matador. I am up hear on buisness concirning our new town. I have [two] lots in town & my land is a bout 3 miles from town. I think we will have a good town as we have a good countrie a round & good people.

I have moved from whair I was camped. I am now bording with a familie by the name of Moore. He livs a bout 25 miles Southwest off whaire I was camped & in a bout 12 miles off whair my sister livs.

They was another town run aganst our town for the co. seat but we beat them very bad & Mr. H.H. Campbell is our co. judge. I saw Mr. Turner the day off the Ellection. He run for co. clerk, but dident run much off a race, for he was running a ganst two tirble good boys. Not saying he isent a good man, for I know nothing a bout him only what I hird youal speak off him. He seames to be a nice young man. I also meet Mr. Sammie James at Matador the day after Ellection.

Please excuse this paper as the Post Office is closed & I wouldent have time to write tomorrow. I hope this will find youal well. Direct your next letter, Matador, Texas. When you write to Miss Maggie give hir my regards. I will close with regards to all. I am your true friend.

D.C. Kieth

P. S. Mr. Turner ask me to give youal his best regards.

Feb 24, 1891
(Postmark: Fort Spunky Tex.)

To: Mr. D.C. Kieth
Matador Ranch
Motley Co. Tex.

From: Ft. Spunky Tex.
Feb 23 1891

To: Mr. D.C. Kieth

My truest friend; I have been in receipt of your most welcome favor of Feb. 8th several days & will endeavor to reply to it tonight. Though I havent recd. an answer from my last letter yet, no doubt you have received it by this time.

I am glad indeed to know you was so thoughtful of me, as to write two letters to my one—besides I am glad to hear from you as often as you feel disposed to write. I am glad you are well and having a nice time. And your election was a success. I suppose you all feel some what independent, since you have a county organized.

Well, we farmers are as busy as bees making ready for another crop—corn planting time will be here next week. Pa broke up our garden today, so I'll have the pleasure of planting it soon.

Well! Well! Just think of it; "the dead is alive & the lost is found." The people of this neighborhood met yesterday to organize a Sun. school & a singing class. This is the first move which have been made to that affect here in nearly two years. I have but little confidence in the success of our Sun. school. Ah! You have been to church since you was here. Well, that is more than I can say. I haven't seen a preacher much less having the pleasure of hearing a surmon, since we were at the Springs.

Oh! You just ought to see the two nice free-drawings which I have lately received from an "Arkansas" cousin. One is the "Lords prayer," incircled with a wreath of birds & the other is a family record.

By the way I received a letter from a "Montana" cousin the other day—he is a batchelor of only 35 summers & a stockman. He has been in that business 13 years. He informs me that the girls must not put too much confidence in a Cowboy, nor believe more than half they say. But ah! Don't you think he is rather late in giving his advise—besides I can't agree with him, for I believe the "Cowboys" can & do leave as much honor as any other class of people.

At least, one is esteemed so, in my estimation. But then, he [Montana cousin] said he was only judgeing others by himself.

I am going to tell him if he don't turn over a new leaf, he cant' get a house-keepers, when he gets ready for one, i.e. judging from his advise. I'll close for fear you have already tired of this letter.

This leaves us all very well & hope it will find you enjoying yourself. Write soon & often to your far away but true friend.

Ella

P. S. Dan didn't have the dreaded small pox. He is here but don't know what he intends doing.

E. E. C.   Goodnight.

Feb 24, 1891
(Postmark: Matador Texas)

To: Miss Ella Cribbs
F.T. Spunky
Hood Co. Texas

From: Matador, Texas
Feb 20 1891

To: Miss Ella Cribbs

My tru friend. I recieved your kind & most welcome letter off the 6th and the 17th. It was certainly read with cear & I was so sorrow to hear youal was sick. I do hope & trust this letter will find youal well. I am well at this time. Though when I was sick I just thought a person dident know how to injoy good health untill they got sick. I do trust & pray that youal air well at this time.

I written you a short letter from Estacado severl days ago. I supose you have gotten it by this & from the way your last letter reads, I supose it found youal sick. You dont know how sorrow I feel for youal. Yes, I was very much surprised to hear that Dan was at home. I dident run for Sherrif for I didnt think it would pay much the first tirm. I should gotton it. I do believe I would off gotton the office if I had run. The two Boys that run, run a clost race. One beat the other 3 vots. I believe I told you in my last letter a bout moving my camp & I am well pleased with the exchange. As we have company to neight I wil half to close & finish to morrow neight. So Good neight.

Feb. 23

I will try & finish my letter this eave. This is one a moung the windest ernings I ever saw. I caught my horse this morning to wride & the wind got so high I postponed wriding untill after noon. So it is after noon now & the wind is still very high. So I gess I will not wride any this ear. I met Mr. Wells at Childress with a wagon, so I came out with him. He was the man that was to bring my horse to Teepee. Though he hadent got my letter before he left him. Mr. Wells was at the depot when the train run up, expicting me to be on it. So when I met him he ask me whair was my wife. I told him I couldent persuade hir to come. When I started to Hood Co. Mr. Wells carried me to Childress & I told him if I came back a mairried man then he need not be surprised. So he littled surprised me to bring some one back. He is the man I bourded with last winter.

I am bording with a man by the name of Moore this winter & they air very nice & clever people. They havent any children, though Mr Moores Sister is staying with them & she is very prity & very livly. She is 17 years off age. Hir name is Miss Lillian Moore. She only came a few days ago from Young Co. & gess She will stay untill a bout the first off May. I ask hir how She thought She would like to live in this countrie. She sed She thought She would like to live hear if she was mairred. We all went to a dance & Supper last Wednesday neight. The dance was at one off the Matador Farmers. It was shure a good & nice dance & lasted from a bout 4 p.m. untill 9 a.m., had a large crowd bouth men & women.

Though I think that will be my last dance for this winter & I may never dance any more. Though I dont say I will never dance any more. If I should ever mairrie a women that dosent dance, unless she wants to go to dances, I dont think we will attend many of them. For I dont much believe in mairried people going to dancies any way, espeshly when they air poor like my Self, for it taken money to attend dancies. I know I am not stingy. What I have goes to prove that, for I have ben getting wages for severl years & haven't saved but very little.

I dont gamble & drink but very little, the way I have written those 2 lines a bove sounds like I gamble & drink bouth, but I dont gamble atal. I have enough to settle down & make a very good living, provided I can keep my health & I am very thankfull for it. I have ben blessed with good health the most off my life.

Well, this countrie is beganing to show grean spots in low places. It wil not be long untill we will have plenty off grean grass. I think we will Start out on the range, a bout the first off April, then our sollad neights Sleep will be over for severl, as we will half to stand neight gard off & on the Spring & faul through. I think

I will have the shiping contrack a gan this year, though it will not comens before some time in June.

Please excuse mspelts words. I send regards to all & My Love to you. Write soon to your tru friend.

D.C. Kieth

Apr 7, 1891

(Postmark: Fort Spunky, embossed shield on lined notepaper.)

To: Mr. D.C. Kieth
Matador,
Motley Co. Texas.

From: Ft. Spunky Texas
April 6 1891

To: Mr. D.C. Kieth
Matador Texas

My most esteemed friend; I will try to write a few lines this afternoon, as I havn't had a letter from you since the last of Feb. If you have wrote your letter is undoubtly a long time a coming, at least I have looked for a letter several mails, but was disappointed. March 11th was the date of my last letter to you. Doubtless you have received it by this time. At least I hope so.

I suppose you have met Dan by this time—he left here the 25th of Mar. bound for the Matador ranch. We hav'nt heard from him since he left—though we looked for a letter last mail, but it never came.

Pa and I went to see Maggie last Sat. and of all cold disagreeable rides I ever had, it surealy was the worst. And don't you think! instead of us going to Sun. school, the next morning Maggie & I went calling, and then did't get half way round. We called at "Mrs. Dr. Walkers" & behold I met Mr. Jno. B. Estes there. He informed us he would start for the extreme west, next week.

Maggie sends her kindest regards to you & her thanks for yours to her. I will close as I hav't any letter to ans. nor any news & interest to write. This leaves us well & hope it will find you the same. Please write soon & often to your true friend.

Ella

My best wishes to thee.

Apr 9, 1891

(Postmark: Teepee City Tex)

To: Miss Ella Cribbs
F. T. Spunky
Hood Co. Texas

From: Teepee City Texas
April 7 1891

To: Miss Ella Cribbs

My dearest friend, I take pleasure to neight in trying to answer you most kind & welcom letter I recieved severl days ago. I trust you will forgive me for not ansern sooner for I have ben so buisy evr since I recieved your letter. I haven't had time to do any thing only work.

We air now gathern our horses to comens our spring work. I think we will began work on the range the 15th. Dan isent at work yet, though I think he will go to work a bout the 15th. I don my best to get his wages started at once but failed, as the Company wont hire any one till work begans. Dan is well ceard for. Youal must not be uneasy a bout him. I saw him to day. He is well & I think very well pleased.

I will half to make a short letter out off this one as it is late at neight now & I have no time to write in day time. Yes, I believe we have agreed on evry thing & I do trust we will continue to do so. They isent a day pass but what I think off you as my truest friend & I trust you have the same thought off my self.

If I hold the shiping contrack it will last untill a bout the 15th off Nov. next, though we will not began to ship beaf cattle till some time in June. I will bring this dull & short letter to a close, asking you to for give me for not writing a longer letter. I hope I will have time to write more next time. I send good wishes to all & remain your truest friend. I trust I may hear from you agan soon. So good neight.

As ever, your truest friend,

D. C. Kieth

Apr 13, 1891

(Postmark: Matador, Texas, "Glenwood" embossed on note paper)

To: Miss Ella Cribbs
F. T. Spunky
Hood Co. Texas

From: Matador Texas
April 17 1891

To: Miss Ella Cribbs

My dearest friend I take much pleasure in trying to answer your kind & most welcome letter off Apr the 6th & was certainly glad to hear from you a gan & hear youal was well. I recieved your last letter last Wednesday eve. I am sorrow you had to wait so long for an answer to your letter off Feb. 11th but couldent well help it, as I have ben so buisy for the last two mounths.

I trust you will forgive me, wil you not. It wasent because I dident want to write by any means, for I am always glad when I have the pleasure & opportunity off writing to you. I writen to you from Teepee City. I think it was the 7th off this mounth, so I supose you have gotten my letter by this time. I hope you have, at least. I am glad to know you think so much off me as to write a gan with out an answr from my letter.

I am always glad to hear from you. I only wish I could write to you & hear from you evry week, though it will be most impossible for me to write very often from now on, as I will be so buisy at work. Though I will promis to write as often as I can & I hope to hear from you as often as you wish to write.

The manager off the ranch is talking off having me to cow hunt this year, so if he does, I will have a poor chance to get my mail for a mounth or two at the time. If you fail to get an answr from any of your letters to me for some time, please do not think strange off it for it will not be my fault.

I would not off had the chance off writing to day, but it has ben raining so hard all day we couldent get out to do any thing. We air so luckey to be at the ranch at this time. We will start out on the range to work just as soon as the rain is over. They is a large number off us boys at the ranch today. Dan has comens work for this company. He is well & well pleased.

You will please excuse pencil & poor writing as I have a poor way to write. I am off in the harness shop by my self trying to write. I do hope & trust I will be able to live at home next year & make my living with out cow hunting, wich I think I can, provided I keep my health.

I was sorrow to know you & your father had such a disagree-able ride to the Thorp Springs, though was glad to know you & Miss Maggie had such a nice time calling. You spoke off Mr. J.B. Estes starting for the West. Do you know what part off the West he was going to? I have a cousin at Matador, keeping books for Judge Campbell. He is from Jacksboro, Jack Co., Texas. His name is Atkinson. If my relations keep coming out I will have several off them in this countrie after a while, so I am glad to see them come. The Matador town is one mile north off the ranch.

We air having the finest rain we have had for severl mounths in this countrie. The grass will come very fast after it is over & I think the farmers will make good crops. I hope so any way. I expect to be a farmer a moung them next year. I think I have got post enough to fence a good feal & a garden & a yard, wich I intend doing next summer. I have a good well on my land & good soft water, wich I think is two thirds off the badle [battle].

Your father wrote me he was coming out next summer to look at the countrie. I hope he will come & hope he will be satisfied with our countrie & find him a good pease off land. Some ses this will be a good farming countrie & some ses it wont, so I dont know my self but I intend on trying it. Though I dont expect to depend on farming al together, so if I fail at one thing probly I will succeed at an other. They is severl new farms opeing up out hear this year.

Well, I will bring this porly written letter to a close, for I know you will get tired trying to read it. This leaves Dan & I well & I trust it will find youal well. I send good wishes to all & my love to you. Write soon & often to your truest friend.

D.C. Kieth

May 7, 1891
(Postmark illegible)

To: Mr. D.C. Kieth
~~Matador~~
Forwarded: Teepee City
Motley Co. Tex.

From: Ft. Spunk Texas
May 6 1891

To: Mr. D.C. Kieth,
Matador Tex:

My dear friend; I will write you a few lines tonight not with-standing, you are due a letter. I received your handsome photo last week--& deem it deserves an answer. Rest assured it was an agree-able surprise to me indeed. Please accept my thanks for it. I am delighted to know you remembered me when you had them made. I regret very much I cant return the compliment at present, sending you mine but hope you will not feel much disappointed.

We are up so nicely with our work—we finished hoeing the corn last week, I suppose you all are quite busy as well as us farm-ers. We, i.e. Carrie & I, are spending this week visiting, making soap, washing, ironing, scouring & etc. etc. Excuse me please for telling you such trifles.

Monday, I went to see friends whom live one mile beyond where we attended that party Xmas night. They are begging me to teach school for them next summer—though they will spend July visiting relatives in Ohio. At the same time I didnt promise to teach for them.

Oh! I thought so many times Monday, while riding across the prarie, what a lovely time you all must be having, i.e. if you have to cow hunt alone. Though I enjoy a horse back ride if it is all alone.

O Sunday is preaching Sun. Come & enjoy the sermon with us? Besides we have so many pretty flowers, the rose bushes looks like boquetts. I recond you have lots of wild flowers which are as pretty as our cultivated ones.

Our Sunday school isn't as interesting as it ought to be. The majority of the people here seem to be carless in retgard to religious duties—it seems like they ough[t] to know that "we must reap as we have sown." What has become of Dan? We haven't had a letter from him in three weeks? We are having some real cool weather this week, for May. I will close as evry one is in bed but me & the lamp flys is so provoking, and doubtless, you are already tired of this uninteresting letter any way. I trust this will find you & Dan well.

Please excuse all mistakes & write soon to your faraway but true friend.

Ella

May 16, 1891
(Postmark: Teepee City Tex., capitol building
embossed on note paper.)

To: Miss Ella Cribbs
F. T. Spulky
Hood Co) Texas

From: Teepee City, Texas
May 15 1891

To: Miss Ella Cribbs

My dearest friend. It is with much pleasure I try to answer your two last letters I recieved day before yesterday & can say they was read with much pleasure, over and over again. I was glad to learn youal was well. I am well at this time. I hird from Dan to day. He was well & well pleased. Youal must not be uneasy about him, though when I see him I will tell him he aught to write home oftener, for I know youal would like to hear from him often.

Well, I will not half to cow hunt as far from home this year as I thought I would. Teepee City I supose will be my post office, now for some time & I think I will have a chance to get my mail prity regular. When I am out on a hunt, I make my head quarters on Toung [Tongue a.k.a. South Pease] River at a famlies by the name of Austins. They air mity nice & clever people. They air farming for the Company. Mr. Wells livs 3 miles a bove this place on the river, so he farms for the Company two. Mr. Austin has a neace living with him by the name of Miss Ellen Caltharp.

Just as soon as cow hunting is over, I want to go to work on my land & improve all I can through Augst. & then they want me to cow hunt for them a gan next faul.

I will change the subject. I believe our time is set for July isent it. Though if you will agree with me, I would like to lenthing the time till next winter, but if that isent agreable with you, I will make my word good, as I am a poor man. I think it would best for us to wait till next winter, as I believe I can get fixed by that time. So I can be at home the most off my time. Please do not dout me because I ask to put the time till next winter. Yes, Miss Lillian has gone home.

They was a man killed at the ranch a few days ago.[79] He left a wife & two little children & I feel so sorrow for them, for they air very poor. I just returned from a hunt 3 days ago & expect will

---

79. Wagon boss Jeff Varner was killed by J.B. Mcleod at the Matador Ranch headquarters on May 10, 1891. Potts, Marisue. *Motley County Roundup: Over 100 Years of Gathering* Second Edition (Matador, Texas: Mollie Burleson Ranch Ltd., 2020), pp. 103, 132.

start outt a gan Monday. I will half to close as it is getting late at neight. I send good wishes to all. I will write a gan the first chance I have. So write soon & often to your truest friend,

D.C. Kieth
Good neight.

May 25, 1891
(Postmark: Teepee City Tex.)

To: Miss Ella Cribbs
F. T. Spunky
Hood Co. Texas

From: Teepee City Texas
May 25 1891

To: Miss Ella Cribbs
My dearest & nearest friend.

It is with greatest pleasure I take this earning in trying to write you a few more lines, though I am afraid you will get dis-justed at my writing. So often for my self I wish I cuid hear from you or see & talk with you every day, for you seam nearer & dearer to me than any one living.

I have jist finish work through one pasture & will start to an-other one in a bout 3 days, to bee gone a bout one week. When I return from that work, I think probly I will get to rest 2 or 3 days. I hird from Dan yesturday. He was well. The outfit he is with is camped a bout three miles from this place. I met one off the boys yesturday, as I was crosing the prarie, that works with Dan. They air lying over at present, though I think they ame to start to branding a bout the 1st of June. I past in a bout 2 hundred yards off thair wagon yesturday ear. But didnt have time to stop. We air having the finest rains this year, so for than we have had for seval.

I will half to make a short letter out off this one, as I havent but little time to write. So I will close for this time sending love & best wishes to you & also wish to hear from you soon. Your truest friend as ever,

D.C. Kieth

June [6?], 1891
(Postmark: Teepee City Tex.)

To: Miss Ella Cribbs.
F.T. Spunky
Hood Co) Texas

From: Teepee City, Texas
June 2 1891

To: Miss Ella Cribbs,

My Dearest friend, you have no ida how happy I am to know I have the pleasure off ansern another letter from home [whom] I love best on earth. I am glad to hear youal air well, though I believe you written your mother wasent very well. I trust this letter will find youal well. I havent ben feealing very well for the past few days, though I feeal verry well today.

I just returned from a hunt last Sunday eav. but think I will half to start out a gan some time next week. I am sorrow to know you work so hard. I know it is because you air so kind & wiling to help your Father. I trust thair will be rest & happyness in the feauther [future] for youal. I recieved your kind & most welcom letter this eave & redit with much pleasure & cear. I written to your Father last neight & came over to mail my letter to day & found your letter awaiting at the office for me, though I was wishing as I came a long I would find a letter hear from you. So, I am glad I can say I got my wishes one time. I know you al will be glad to see Miss Maggie come home for she has ben away so long. Tell hir hidy for me.

I am glad to know you put so much confidence in my self. I can only return the same to you. My love for you is greater than any one on earth. So, I think it should be on boath sids, dont you? The reason I dident set any mounth in my last letter, I thought I had rather wait until I hird from you a gan. So I will say December next, providing that mounth will be ageable with you. So, if it is, you will please set the day. Do you wish me to write to your Father & Mother in regard to our ingagement, or shall I wait until I come down?

I will change the subject. The next day after I written my last letter to you, I met Dan & had a long talk with him. He seams to be well pleased. They started the next day out on the plains to start to branding. Well, I must close for this time as it is getting late. I send my good wishes to all & my love to you. Write soon & often to your loving friend.

D.C. Kieth

Jun 1[4], 1891

(Postmark: Teepee City Tex.)

To: Miss Ella E. Cribbs.
F. T. Spunky,
Hood Co) Texas.

From: Teepee City Texas
Jun 14 1891

To: Miss Ella E. Cribbs

My Dearest. It is with much pleasure I attempt to write you a few lines this pleasant Sun eav. I am well at this time & I trust those few lines will find youal well. I haven't hird from Dan since I written to you last. I think they air some whaire on the south side off the pasture.

We have had the hardest rains hear in the past 10 days we have had for seveal years. The rains & wind don som damage in this countrie but not to much, though we hear they has ben seveal drownded persons found in the lower countrie. I supose the river clost to youal got very high. The man I am bourding with has a good crop off corn & wheat & oats. His corn feal is clost to the river & waters got all over the feal & disstroid a gradeal off the corn. His wheat & oats was on higher ground so it dident damage them much. I have ben fixen up water gaps for the past week. So, I have got them all fixed.

I will start to marrow out on another cow hunt to be gone a bout 10 days, though I will not be very far from my head quarters at any time on this trip. I am at Mr. Welles to day, so he sed he would be going to Teepee some time this week. I thought I *would drop you a few lins & let you know I am still on the land off the living.*

I trust this letter will find you injoying your self. Do you think your Father will come out next mounth or not? I haven't hird from him for seveal days. Well, as it is getting late in the ear. & I half to go back to my bourding place, I will come to a close.

By the way, plums air getting ripe & we have a grate many this year. I wish you wear hear so we could go plum hunting. Do you Like plums? I will close hoping this will find youal well. Write soon to your tru & loving friend forever.

D.C. Kieth

June 30, 1891
(Postmark: Teepee City, Tex., capital building
embossed on note paper)

To: Miss Ella Cribbs
F. T. Spunky
Hood Co. T_____ [torn]

From: Teepee City. Texas,
June 29 1891

To: Miss Ella Cribbs

My dearest & true friend. I take greate pleasure to neight in writing you a few lines in anser to your kind letter I recieved a few days ago. I am well at this time & trust those few lines may find youall well.

I saw Dan to day. He is well. Dan is working with the branding outfit & I am with the beaf outfit at present. I havent time to write but a few lines to neight as it is late & we air working very hard evry day.

We air camped clost to Teepee to neight & they air seveal off us boys up at the store & they air hurrin me to go. I cant hardly write any way for them talking and lafing. Probly I will get chance to write you a long letter in a few days.

No, they wasent any off those men that drownded Matador men.

I will close this time. With good wishes to youall & my love to you. Please excuse this short & dull letter & write soon. Your true friend,

D.C.K.

[July] 13, 1891
(Postmark Torn: C[hildress], Tex)

To: Miss Ella Cribbs.
F. T. Spunkey.
Hood Co.) Texas.

From: Childress
Childress Co. Texas
July 12 1891

To: Miss Ella Cribbs

My dearest Girl. A gan I take my pencil in hand at one off my lonsoms hours to write you a few lines. Though I [feel] very dull as I have ben travling for the past two days & neights & have had but very little sleep. I landed at this plce this morning a bout 9 oclock, from a trip to Kansas and will start for the ranch in the morning. Most off the young people in this town has gone to church as to day is Sunday. But I dident feel like going my self & as I was thinking off you. I though[t] I could pass off the time better & more pleasanter writing to you than any thing I could do or any whair I could go.

This is a beautiful & lovly day & I hope you air having a nice time. I written to you from Degraff, Kansas and epect this letter will reach you a bout as soon as that one does. So, if you get them bouth at once I know you will get worried trying to read them.

I will change my subject. The Company I am working for wants me to live on the east side off the range & look after the joining pasturs, though I have never told them wheather I would or not. But, if I should make such a trade with them, would it be agreeable with you? Why I ask you this question is because I think it is right I should. I dont want to try to make you think I aim to do one way & you do another. Though if I would make that kind off trade with them, I didn't intend on living in the house with any one else. They will be furning [furnishing] us a house to live in & in another year probably I would be able to fix our home up better than I could at presant. Now, I am just only sugjusting this to you. Dont know yet for cirtain how I will do but want to do what evr is the best for us if I can.

Well, as I feel so slepy & dull I will bring this letter to close & think I shall put in most off this ear. sleeping. Well, what do think by this time a bout your Father coming out? Do you think he will come or not? If he does I hope he will come some time in this mounth or next & probly I can assist him some in going a round & looking at the lands. I trust may find youal well. Write soon & often to your truest & loving friend.

As ever

D.C. Kieth

P.S. I will put another sheat off paper a round this as the writing shows through [envelope]

July 19, 1891
(Postmark illegible)

To: Miss Ella Cribbs
F.T. Spunkey
Hood Co. Texas

From: Degraff Kansas
July 10 1891

To: Miss Ella Cribbs

My dearest and true friend. It is with greate pleasure I take this beautiful morning in writing you a few more lines, to let you know I am still on the lands off the livings, though I am a distain from whair I was when I last written to you. When I writen to you I hadent much ida off taken this trip. I landed at this place yesturday earning with safty & will start back to Texas this [rail] car. I shipped a train off cattle to this place wich is to be pastured here until faul & then shipped to market. The blue stem grass is very fine in this country. This is a farming countrie & a stock countrie combied [combined] & the people have made good crops through the most of the countrie I have seean.

I will change my subject. When I writen to you last, as well as can remember, I neglected to give you an answer concirning the date of our mairriage. I trust you will forgive me for being so cearles. So, I believe you set the 24th day off Dec. next & ask if that day would suit me. Cirtainly, it will, though as you sed in your last letter, when or before that time comes it might suit eather off us to set some other date. If so, I trust & believe it will be agreable with bouth, fur I think enough off you to wait until the last hour.

You air my daly thoughts & seam nearer & dearer to me than any one on earth, wich I think we aught to be to each another concidern circumstances, dont you? I know or at least believe you do. Yes, I do wish it was so we could see each other evry day, for as you say we could talk more in an ouer [hour] than could be writen in one day. Athough I am a very poor talker, I think I could talk to you more & better than I could to any one else.

Just to think I was the most unlukiest man on earth, but it is just the other way with me now. My feauther [future] days seams bright, weather they air or not. Though I trust & believe they air, so I will live in hopes if I die in disspair. I aim to build a *house this summer & expecet will go to holing my lumber when I return to ranch, as I want to build some time next mounth if I can.*

Well, I will come to a close for this time. Hoping to hear from you soon. I am well & trust this will find youal. Well, regards to all. I am your tru & loving friend for ever & ever.

D. C. Kieth

July 21, 1891

(Postmark: Becton Texas)

To: Miss Ella Cribbs
F. T. Spunky
Hood Co. Texas

From: Matador
Motley Co. Texas
July 19 1891

To: Miss Ella Cribbs

My dearest & loving litter friend.

It is with greate pleasure I attemp to answer your kind & most welcom letter I recieved a few days ago. This leaves Dan & I well & trust it will find youal well. Dan & my nephew has gone to church & also my two neases [nieces]. Sister & I & the litter ones stayed at home & got dinner. I dident cear to go to church my self, as I hadent ben hear since early last spring until a bout 3 days ago. So, I thought I had rather stay at home & talk withe Sister than go to church. We camped a bout 12 miles south off hear. We are taking a few days rest spell though I think they air intending on us to go to work a bout the 20th, but I dont think we can work much untill it rains. We may not comens until it does rain, for we are begun to need rain a gan very bad. Had a light shower last night, but not to do much good. Dan & I will go back to camps this evning.

Well, the Girls & Dan & Willie has come from Sunday school. They dident have any preching. My oldest neace is 17 years old & the other one 14. The olest name is Bettie & the other name is Myrtle & 2 litter Girls named Muriel & Pirl. Sister ses your mother aught to come with your Father if he comes in a wagon as it would be most shure to improve hir health. I hope this will find youal well. Pleas excuse this short letter & write soon to your truest & loving friend.

D.C. Keith

Aug 11, 1891

(Postmark: Fort Spunky Tex, top one-third
of letter folded to a point)

To: Mr. D.C. Kieth
Teepee City
Motley Co. Texas

From: Ft. Spunky Tex.
Aug 9 1891

To: Mr. D.C. Kieth

Teepee City

My most kind and dear friend: it affords me much pleasure to find my self trying to asn. You most welcome letter wich I have been in receipt of for several days. I am sorry I am on the tardy sort, but can you forgive me this time? We have so much company for the past two weeks & have been visiting considerably ourselves.

My married sister & family is here & they have all gone to church on the Georgia's [George's] Creek, accept for Pa and my self. I stayed at home to write to you & cook dinner. I may go to church this afternoon, as there will be preaching at the school house.

I am real glad you & Dan had a nice time visiting your sister. I supose he is having too fine a time to write to us. We havent had a letter from him since I wrote to you last. I supose you have recd. my last letter ere this time. I felt some what disappointed last evening when the mail was called & no letter from you to me—But recond you havent had time to write as you said you would begin work on the 20th. Some of our young men is in on a rest & they look like they need it. When one of them arrived at Ft. Worth, on his way back from shiping beeves, he said he coudnt go on to the ranch without paying his relatives & friends a visit when he was so near. Now he says he dont think he can ever to back to the ranch, as he is having such a fine time here, compared to the lonely time out there.

It seems as though evry one is having a nice time here this summer, attending picnics, weddings, parties & protracted meetings. Protracted meetings has been in session for the past 3 weeks & I expect they will last 3 weeks longer.

It has clouded up & looks like it will rain in a few minutes. I hope you have a good rain by this time. There is a good prospect for a good cotton crop at present. My brother in-law says we have bale per acre now--& just think, it is beginning to open now.

We have just organized a nice literary society, which is in session each Fri. eve. after school. Maggie is president & I am secretary & Carrie is second critic. You and Dan come & join us next Fri. evenings. Please excuse all mistakes & this hastily writen letter. Write as soon & as often as you can to your truest,

Ella

Aug 18, 1891
(Postmark: Childress Tex.)

To: Miss Ella Cribbs
F. T. Spunky
Hood Co. Texas

From: Teepee City, Texas
Aug 15 1891

To: Miss Ella Cribbs
F. T. Spunky

My Dearest & loving Girl. You have no ida how glad I am when I have he pleasure & opirtunity off writing to you. Yes, I have red your last letter seveal days ago, but havent had any chance to answer untill now & only have a few minutes to write in this eavening. Will you forgive me? I know you will, for I have ben so buisy ever since the 22nd off July. Though I am [sure] you was disapointed when you went to meet the mail & fail to get a letter from my self. I will write evry chance & I want you to do the same.

You air my dayly thoughts. I often think if it was so we could see each other evry day I would be as happy as I want to be, though I will live in hopes if I die in disspaire, If it wasent for hopes if the feauther [future], I don't know what would become off a poor man like my self. You ask me to forgive you for not answer sooner. Cintainly, I will.

I recieved your letter off the 9th yesturday eave, but hadent time to answer while at [post] office, as I got thaire very late. I had ben running a bunch off wild horses all day & was very tired. So, I coreld the horses after so long a time & brought them to camps to day.

The outfit Dan works with was camped near Teepee last neight. So, I stayed all neight with them. Dan is well & seams to be well pleased. The man he is working for thinks a greadeal off him. We have at this time 17 hundred head off beaf cattle under hurd. I think we will start for the rail road with them next Tuesday & expect I wil half to go off with them. If I do, I will be gone a bout 9 days & it will take us a bout 3 days to go to the road, wich will be 12 or 13 days in all.

Your father writen like he might get out hear some time be-tween the 15th & 20th. Dan ses if his Father dosent com this summer he [Dan] will take up a section next winter & hold it until [his father] can come. So, he can do that very easy if he will. I have a good section & a good well off water on it, but dont know yet weather I will live thaire next winter or not. Havent had any talk with [Mr] McKinzy [Murdo Mackenzie] a bout the matter lately. I think he is coming out to our camp to morrow & will probly have some under standing with him before he goes back home. He lives in Trinidad, Colorado. He is Superintendent off this ranch.

You wanted to know if I made a trade with him to live on the east side off the range. If I would be gone on those protracted hunts, know [now] dont think I would evr be gone more than 5 or 6 days at the time. I would never half to go [except] for only work in join- ing pasturs, though I may be able to fix so I can stay at home very near all the time.

I will if I can, but as I am a pore man, I will just half to do the best I can. That is all I can do, but probly we may get fix some day so we can fix up better than I can at this time. I hope & trust we may. Now you may get very lonely out here at times for this isent a settled countrie a tal to compare with that countrie, but will never leave you a day longer by your self than I can help. Now I want you to think all that over & be satisfied you air wiling to come & help me climb the hill, wich I believe you air, why I explained this to you—if you should come out here with me & get dssatisfied I would be so sorrow, so I feal it my duty to explain what I have to you.

Well, I will half to come to a close prity soon as it is airy near supper time & I am a bout one half mile down on a creek below camps trying to write to you. 3 other men & my self will half to take charge off the cattle after supper.

I send good wishes to all. Tell Miss Maggie hidy for me. Write soon & often. I am your tru & loving friend for ever & ever. So good by, My dearest Girl.

D.C. Kieth

Aug 20, 1891
(Postmark illegible)

To: Miss Ella Cribbs
F. T. Spunky
Hood Co. Tex

From: Giles[80] Texas
Aug 20 1891

To: Miss Ella Cribbs

My dear girl. I take my pencil in hand to neight to try & write you a few lines, hoping they may find youal well. I am well at this time. Well, we air near the rail road to neight & think we will ship to marrow, that is, if the cars comes so we can load our cattle. We have had very good luck coming up the trail so far.

Well, I cant think of much to write to neight. The Boys has all gone to bed except my self & 2 that is on first gard. I am sitting by my lantern trying to write to one who seames so dear to me. When I came in to supper this earning & was unsadling my horse I thought off you & thought I would like to write you a few lines to neight as it might be seveal days before I would get a chance to write, though I will write to you from Chigago [Chicago] if it is so I can.

Is your Father started out hear a bout the time he thought he would, when he writen last? I gess he is at Mr. Wellses now. I hope I will get back in time to see him if he does come.

---

80. Giles was a Ft. Worth & Denver Railway shipping point with pens, water, and pasture, located in Donley County. The Matador cowboys considered it an unlucky place due to fatalities and accidents that took place there.

Well, I will come to a close. I half to get up at one oclock &
stand till 3. We have ben standing neight gard for very near one
mounth, study [steady]. This is a beautifull neight. I send good
wishes to all & my love to you. So good neight.

Your tru friend,

D.C.

Aug [2_], 1891
(Postmark: Fort Madison Iowa)

To: Miss Ella Cribbs
F. T. Spunky
Hood Co) Texas

From: F. T. Madison, Ioa.
Aug 25, 1891

To: [Miss Ella Cribbs]
My Dearest Girl.

With greate pleasure I attempt to write you a few lines to let
you know whair I am & that I am well. I only trust this will find
youal well.

I landed at this place yesturday ear. & will leave hear at 2
oclock this ear. for Chicago & if have good luck will get to Chicago
a bout 2 oclock to marrow morning. This is a fine countrie. Evry
Body seames to have fine crops in the countrie. I will land back in
Texas about the first, if I have no bad luck, I will close as it [is]

a bout 3 miles from hear to my boarding house & a bout one half mile from thair to the stock pens & tis after 11 oclock now.

I send good wishes to you. I hope & think I will find a letter from you to me when I return to Teepee City. So, I will close for this time. I remain your tru loving friend.

D.C. Kieth

Good by my dear—

Aug 29, 1891

(Postmark: Fort Spunky Tex. postmark forwarded: Teepee City, Sept 4 1891; forwarded: Matador; Faded blue ink is obscured on lined notepaper. Photocopying brings out some text.)

To: Mr. D.C. Kieth
Teepee City
Motley Co. Tex.

From: Ft. Spunky Tex
Aug 27 1891

To: Mr. D.C. Kieth,
Teepee City

Dearest friend, you can't imagine how delighted I was to hear from you. I recd. yours of the 15th inst, first Sat. & the 20th last Tues. Oh! It would make time seem so much shorter, if I could always hear from you each mail. But I know you can't write that often while you are so busy, though I am confident you will always write as often as you can & I will prompaly ans. all your letters. Each of your letters always brings me a nice compliment & praises of the highest degree. Now will you accept mine in return?

I pray that I will always be & [we] prove to be as dear & true to each other as we are at present. I know I am not as well accomplished in the arts as some young ladies is—but as you have made choicing me to share your future, I willingly do all I can to help make our home happy. I think there is a great many things conneced with this word "Home," perhaps more than many prac- tice or seem to understand. I don't claim to know the subject thor- oughly, but I think it is something more than a square inclosed with four walls.

Did you understand from my last letter that I wasn't will- ing to go to the beautiful west with you? I know it will be a little lonesome to me there, compared with this country. But the best of [illegible] someday. We have a great deal of company & there I don't have much time to get lonesome in [illegible] way.

The Free Will Baptist is holding a meeting at the school house (this week). I haven't attended many times as we are busy picking cotton. We commenced 4 days sooner tis year than we ever did. We ar trying to pick a bale while Pa is gone; he started for the west the 24th. I hope he will meet you & Dan. I think it kind in Dan in the offer he made Pa. Also in you in lending a helping hand in showing him over the country. Several of our neighbors asked Pa to look out for them a location too.

We all recd. letters from Dan last Sat. He said he [enjoyed] his visit to your sisters "splendidly." I am glad Dan's boss likes him. Who is his boss? Dan also says "he is working with a nice set of [cow] boys."

I am glad you was well & had good luck on the trail & hope good fortune will ever smile on you. I suppose you are in or on your way from Chi[c]ago today. I wish you a pleasant trip. I will quit for today, as 'tis nearly time to go to the field & will finish tomorrow.

Aug. 28th

I will finish your letter to day. We will pick cotton this afternoon as school closed today & we wish to attend the closing exercises, besides the teacher wishes us to assist in the recitations. Carrie & I have picked 677 lbs. of cotton this [week?]. We are needing rain badly.

Oh! I formed the acquaintance of two [sweet?] girls of Comanche Co., while they were visiting relatives in this neighborhood, but they started home last Monday.

I trust this letter will meet you with a welcome at the [post] office when you come back.

Will close as dinner is ready. Maggie sends her kindest regards to you. Please excuse all mistakes & scribbling—my fingers are very sore from being stung by the nettles in the cotton. Write as often as you can. As ever yours,

Ella

"Like sweet music pealing
Far o're the deep sea
Oft comes o're me stealing
Sweet memories of thee."

Aug 30, 1891
(Postmark: Childress Tex.)

To: Miss Ella Cribbs
F. T. Spunky
Hood Co) Texas

From: Childress, Texas
Aug 30 1891

Miss Ella Cribbs

My Darling Girl. It affords me much pleasure to write you a few more lines to let you know I turned back to Texas with safety, landed hear yesturday. I will go out to Teepee to day whaire I expect to find the out fit camped, but the outfit Dan is with I think is camped a bout 20 miles south west off Teepee. I dont think they air ronding [rounding up cattle] now, but think they will commens a bout the 15th.

A man by the name off McDonal[81] works on the Matador Ranch. He will take the train this morning for your countrie, whaire he ses his wife is. I believe he sed she was some whaire on Gorgies Creek[82] He is going down to move his family out to this countrie. By the way, I learn hear that your Father has don gone out to my countrie. So, I wil get to see him in a few days. I do hope he wil like and find him a good peace of land, for that is certainly a good healthy countrie.

---

81. D.E. McDonald received his first pay voucher from the Matador Ranch on April 25, 1885, with "Mrs. Macdonald" listed on February 1889, according to *Matador Ranch Cowboy List, Start Dates*, Southwest Collection, Texas Tech Library, Lubbock, Texas. Accessed on 08/01/1994 from j:/public/records/mat-list.doc.

82. George's Creek joins the Brazos River near Fort Spunky where Ella's family farmed.

I am satisfied it would improve your mothers health to come out hear. Sister sed your father ought to off come in a wagon & brought your mother with him. Sister had a greate laugh on me when I was up thaire. I put all confidence in hir, in telling hir anything, for I concider hir my best friend on earth except for your self. One of hir litter Girls a bout 4 or 5 years old was in the room & hird us talking a bout you & myself & after a while the litter Girl ses, "Uncle D, you must bring Aunt Ella up to see us." I dont believe I evr sean any one laugh any heurtier than Sister did. So I told hir alright we would come up to see them. The litter Girls name was Pirl Garner & she is the Sweeteast child I ever saw, thinks thaire is no one like my self. I will close as my horse is sadled & ready for me to start. I send good wishes to all & tru & everlasting love to you. So good by, My darling Girl.

D.

P. S. Write soon & a long letter to your tru friend. D.

Sept 16, 1891

(Postmark: Matador, Texas)

To: Miss Ella Cribbs,
F. T. Spunky
Hood Co. Texas

OFFICE OF J.P. BAYLEY, SURVEYOR
MOTLEY COUNTY, MATADOR TEXAS

Sept 8 1891

To: Miss Ella Cribbs

My Dear Girl, I take greate pleasure this eav. in writing you a few lines in answer to your kind & most welcome letter off the 20th off last mounth. I found your letter at Mr Halies down on Toung River (Tongue River a.k.a. South Pease) last Sunday eav, & it was read with much pleasure. You have no ida how much comford it gives me to read a letter from you.

Your Father seam to be in love with this countrie. I carried him down to Mr Halies Sunday & I think he aims to start home Tuesday. He had a tirble coal the last 2 ora 3 days he was hear, but think he was better Sunday eave. I hope he will return home with safty & find youal well. Dan & I air well at this time. Your Father is going to live on my section next year & improve some for me. I have ben at work on my land for the last few days. Your Father sed he would move out this faul if he could. So, I do hope he will. I think youal will like this countrie & think it will help your mothers health. At least I hope that it will.

No, I dident understand from any off your letter that you wasent wiling to come out hear with me, but thought it my deauty to write to you in the way I did, not that I douted you in the least. For I place all confidence in you. If I writen in any way that hirt your feealings I beg you to forgive, for you air more than all the world to me. Thaire is no one seams so dear. I spoke to your Father a bout our mairriage while he was out hear so he sed thair was no objections. You may think I was rather hasty, but I thought it best as he was intending on moving out hear this faul, if he could get ready before winter, & then he would know better what to depend on.

Whair we will live this winter will be about 15 miles from my section, but think we will be able to live at home after next year.

Your Father talked like he might only bring some off youal out this faul & the rest come next Spring. I hope you will come with him this faul, for it will be better for us, for I will not be able to lose any more time than I can help & we can get mairried out hear. I will be ready to welcom you home at any time if we should chouse to shorting the time we have set. I hope you will not think strange off me writing the way I have, for I am firm & honest in evry line I have writen. I think it would be best as I am a pore man & half to work hard for a living. Please excuse this paper as thaire is no other kind in the office at present. Also excuse mspelt words, for you know I am a pore speller.

Well, I will bring my letter to a close for this time & will write as often as I can & want you to do the same. I send regards & good wishes to all. So good by, my Dear Girl. I am & will be your tru & faithful friend for ever & ever.

D.C. Kieth

P. S. Direct to Teepee City   D.

Sept 15, 1891

(Postmark: Fort Spunky Tex; another faded ink letter)

To: Mr. D.C. Kieth
Teepee City
Motley Co. Tex.

From: Ft. Spunky
Sept 15 1891

To: Mr. D.C. Kieth,
Teepee City, Tex;

My dearest friend, it is with pleasure I'll try to devote a portion of this beautiful Sun. morning in trying to ans. your two last letters. You wrote one while in Iowa & the other at Childress. I had a letter mailed to you two weeks ago yesterday. I suppose you found it at the [post] office when you arrived there.

I am truly glad [all] was well & back in Texas & that you was so kind to write me on those trips. It always affords me much pleasure to receive a letter from you at home or abroad, & I always eagerly accept my opportunity to ans. your most kind letters. Well, I presume the time is fast approaching to close our communications on paper & then I suppose our conversations will be verbaly from hencefourth, til the close of our short stay here on earth.

Not in asking any rough wish for you—but I am glad your sister enjoyed a laugh if it was at your expense. But ah! Those sweet little inosence can always understand elder peoples conversations so much better than we think.

When my sister was here, one of my former admirers called & don't you think Maggie sent the children in to greet him as usual. But as good fortune would have it, they couldn't talk plans, consequently he didn't understand what they said.

Oh! Pa arrived O.K. last Wednesday evening & you can't imagine how glad we were to see him. Carrie said she was so tired feeling after picking cotton all day. We Picked 1½ bales of cotton while Pa was gone. Carrie & I picked 1,549 lbs. last week so I was just too tired to go to Sun. school this morning, but think I will go to church this after-noon.

Oh! We have so much to do to get ready to move by the time Pa wishes to start. I am indeed surprised to know Pa intends to make such a move as this with Ma & by private conveyance & that in the winter. Ma was much anxious to take this trip last summer, but we concluded the weather was too warm & the journey too far for her then.

I never saw any one more delighted with a country & its people than Pa is—with your country. I am confident it would make Pa sick if we should fail to get ready to move out there this year. Mr. T. B. Walsh has just returned & located in Stonewall Co. His eldest son has charge of his ranch. Every few weeks we can hear some one going west with their cattle.

We attended a writing exhibition last night. When our school closed, the assistant teacher taught a writing class at night. We didn't attend, though he specialy invited us. I will close as 'tis dinner time & I wish to write to that dear brother of mine out there, today. Write soon. Most devotedly yours,

Ella

[Sept 29, 1891]
(Postmark: Teepee City Tex)

To: Miss Ella Cribbs
F. T. Spunky
Hood Co Texas

From: Teepee City, Texas
Sep 28 1891

To: Miss Ella Cribbs

My Dear Girl. I am delighted to know I have the opirtunity off answern another letter from you. I recieved your kind & most welcom letter this morning. I haven't had any chance to get my mail untill now for some time, as have ben [on] Wilie outfit. I am at this time working in the branding out fit, the out fit Dan is with. Dont think I will half to ship any more. I am glad to know your Father returned home safe, also glad to know he was so well pleased with this countrie & the people.

I writen to you seveal days ago from Matador. Suppose you have red my letter some days ago. I writen to you in my last letter saying I would like you to come out with your Father this faul. Now you may think I am rather plain asking that off you. So, I am a very plain man, that you air well a wais off. Though if your Mother shouldn't come out this faul & request me to come down their, I will do so according to promis, but do hope youal will move out this faul. Yes, our writing to each other will soon be closed that has ben keep [up] so long & I think I can, but you counting litters when we meet a gan. I believe I have every letter I ever recieved from you but one. You have no idea how dear & near they seame to me, all because you air the writer off them. I was disapointed this morning by not finding a letter hear from your Father, but supose he has ben too buisy telling you a bout this countrie to write.

We have just finished putting up a hurd to start to the rail road. I help to hold the cattle last neight & air on my way back to the branding out fit to day. We will finish work I think a bout the 10th off Nov. I long to see the day when we can see & talk to each other evry day. For I know I will be one a moung the happies men on earth for I do believe I will get one a moung the best women on

earth. I hope & trust your feauther [future] life will be as pleasant & hapy as it seams till be with me. My sister lovs your name
almost as dearly as a sister for she has hird me talk so much off
you & knowing my love for you is so greate. I think she lovs me as
dearly as a Sister coulda brother & I know I love hir as a Brother
could. She was all the world to me until I found they was another
one living so dear.

Well, as I have just a bout 15 miles to ride to make this earning,
I will half bring this letter to a close. Dan is well & well pleased,
so far one to know. I would write to your Father this earning, but it
is so late & would be till some time in the neight [over] taking the
outfit. Probably will [get a] chance to write to him in a few days. I
send good wishes to all. I am & will be your tru & faithful for ever.

D.C. Kieth

P.S. When you see Miss Maggie, shake hands with hir for me.
D.

Oct 3, 1891
(Postmark: Fort Spunky Tex)

To: Mr. D.C. Kieth
Motley Co. Tex.

From: Ft. Spunky Tex.
Oct 1 1891

To: Mr D.C. Kieth
Teepee City;

Dearest friend; as tired as I am tonight, I will try to write you a few lines in response to your last welcome favor which I have been in recept of some 10 days or two weeks. I beg you will excuse me for not writing sooner. Since I have been working so hard, I leave off my writing for Sun. & then we have so much company. Our friends are trying to pay us a visit before we move & Sun. is the only day they have as this is a busy season with us farmers—it looks like it never will rain so we can have an excuse to leave the field. Carrie & I haven't lost a whole day since we commenced picking cotton—we are now picking the 4 bale.

Pa hasn't been well since he came home—but is making his calculations to start [on their journey] about the first of Nov. Ma says we can't leave her behind—she intends to start if she never gets there. She is so in hopes the change will improve her health.

Maggie has decided to go with us too & give up the school she has engaged to teach in Hill County—for it is so sickly down there. My sisters children was exposed to the [w]hoping cough while here last summer & she writes us they all have it. The Dr. has given [up] the eldest, as he has malariah, fever & pneumonia. We did not hear from them last week. They lost their youngest child the 14th of last July.

Quite a serious accident occurred in our neighborhood the 21st of Sept while at a partie two of the boys had a fight & one stabed the other three times—of which he died the following evening. I wasn't at the partie, but attended the funeral & it was the nicest corpse I ever saw. The defendant is on trial this week. The murder[er] cursed his wild, reckless soul & the dying man prayed that his [soul] might be blessed. It seems like this neighbor-hood never will be free of trouble. I am glad Dan isn't here.

Yes, you did right by telling Pa about our marriage & I thank you for your frank explinations & telling me your intentions. I hope we will get off before the winter begins. I expect one of our neighbors will go with us.

Oh! Did you make a confidant of that Mr. McDonald too? Did you tell him about our marriage? I don't remember of ever seeing him—but I've heard a great deal of him & I judge he is no good, so to speak. By the way, Mr. Merriman married a few Sundays ago. I suppose you've recd. my last letter in this time.

Please excuse all mistakes & write soon & I will try to do better next time, so good night.

As ever yours, Ella

Oct 15, 1891

(Postmark: Matador Texas)

To: Miss Ella Cribbs
F. T. Spunky,
Hood Co. Texas

From: Matador Texas
Oct 13 1891

To: Miss Ella Cribbs

My Dearest friend, your letter off Oct 1st came to hand a few days ago & was red with much care. I was glad to hear from you once more & hear youal was well, though I believe you writen your

Father wasent very well. I hope youal air well at this time. Now I have but a little time to write in this earn., hoping you will excuse this haistly writen letter.

We have just finished branding for to day & the outfit has moved a bout 12 miles from hear. We will round to murrow & brand. It is now getting late in the eavening. I am glad to know youal air coming. I do believe coming to this countrie will improve your Mothers health. I hope so any way. I was sorrow to hear off that young man geting kiled. I remember seaning him at the last dance we went to. He seam to be a nice young man.

Yes, I met that Mr McDonal in Childres last summer as I was on my way back from Chigago [Chicago] & he was on his way to Hood Co. At least he told me he was going down thaire after his family. I never did see him but once before & that was last spring. I new nothing a bout him, though he appeared like a very nice Man & claimed he was well acquainted with youal. But when I got to the ranch I learned he had ben arrested out on the plains whaire he was at work. I think papers was sent out thaire from Hood Co. for him for something he had done down thair. Dont know what it was, so I dont think he can ever get work on this ranch any more.

Well, I have always ben onest with you so far as I remember & told you the truth, as well as I could & new how & I believe you have ben the same to me. I believe I did tell McDonal we wear ingaged to be mairried & told him to give youal my regards. Well, [if] I did wrong in telling him any thing, can you forgive me? If not, I will not think any the less off [you], though I hope you can. I hope youal will get off by the 1st anyway & trust you will have a good trip. I want your Father to be shure & come by Garners &

leave youal thair til he can fix up the house. Beshure & write to me a day or so before youal start.

Pleas excuse this paper for it is the best I can do at present. Dan & I air well at this time. By the way, my eldrest neace is to be mairried the 23rd off Dec next. I send good wishes to all. Write soon to your tru friend.

D.C. Kieth

Good by My Dear Girl

Oct 27, 1891
(Postmark: Matador, Texas)

To: Miss Ella Cribbs
F. T. Spunky
Hood Co. Texas

From: Matador Texas
Oct 26 1891

To: Miss Ella Cribbs

My Dearest friend. It is with greate pleasure I attempt to write you a few lines to neight. I received the nice [hair] chain day before yesturday. O, I think it is so nice. Did you make [it] your self. I supose you did. I am sorrow I cant make you a nice birth day presant, but I am not whaire I can get anything. My birth day was the 7th & I believe yours is the 27th, isent it?

I received a letter from you Father day before yesturday. So, he writen that he thought youal would get off in a bout 3 weeks. His letter was dated the 13ᵗʰ. I am a fraid youal will have some bad weather coming out, but I do trust youal will have pirty weather & a nice trip.

We will start to the south side off the range to morrow to comens work to work over the range for the last time this year. We will get back up hear a bout the 12ᵗʰ or 15ᵗʰ off next mounth. I have ben off on a hunt [and] just returned to ranch to day. Dan is well. Please excuse paper and hastley writing. Regards to all. Write soon to your tru friend. Good neight.

D.C. Kieth

P.S.

Please write to me a day or so before youal start. I am at the [post] office to neight, awaiting for the mail. Just trusting I may get a letter from you. **Direct your next letter to Matador.**

How many days do your Father think it will take youal to make the trip? Or have you hird him say? I don't know just how far it is, though I should think it was a bout 250 miles. We call it two hundred miles from hear to Jacksboro. From thair on that way, I dont know the countrie. So, no more at present. D.

Oct 27, 1891

(Postmark smeared: Granb[ury]; postmark on back: Teepee City
Tex.; Oct 30 1891; forwarded to Matador)

To: D.C. Kieth
Teepee City
Motley Co. Texas

From: Ft. Spunky Tex
Oct 19 1891

To: Mr. D.C. Kieth
Teepee City;

My own dear & trust[ed] friend; as "time & tide wait for no one," I most greatefuly accept this pleasant opportunity in trying to write you a few lines in reply to your[s] of Sept the 28th. I am ashamed of my self for not writing sooner, at least, I'll not give any excuse for I know you are tired of reading them. I am ashamed of makeing them.

It seems like it has been an age since I have had a letter from you. I expected a letter from you in last mail but was disappointed. I suppose you are very busy like my self. We finished picking our cotton this after noon. I have only picked 6,800 lbs. At present I can't tell exactly when we can start on our trip. Pa hasn't near finished up his business yet—at the same time, we intend to start just as soon as we can.

Carrie & I anticipate having a nice time & lots of fun on the road. I had my pony broke last summer & she says she intends to ride it out there. I am afraid we will have to go by our selvs, as our friend can't get ready to go with us. I suppose you all will be through with your hardest work by the time we get out there.

Again, I must thank you for your compliments & words are inadequate to express my self for your love & esteem. I pray I will always be worthy of your love & respect & as I have said before, I intend to always try to do my duty in evry respect, though I may fall far short of it. I can heartedly return your sisters most unexpectedly & agreeable compliment, for, you see, she is a near & dear relative of your own dear self.

Yes, you may come if you still wish to, i.e. if we fail to get off. But Pa says he is bound to go this year.

I beg you will excuse this short letter. I would write more but I am not at all well. I have had a headache all day. I am glad you was well & hope this will find you still well. Be sure & write soon & often. As ever your

Ella

Nov 12, 1891

(Postmark: Farmer Tex.; forwarded to Teepee City Txs; sterling notepaper, writing in pencil, which is unusual for Ella)

To: D. C. Kieth
Matador
Motley Co. Texas

From: Jack Co. Tex.
Nov 9 1891

To: Mr. D. C. Kieth,
Matador Tex;

Dear friend;

If I can keep the sand & ashes out of my eyes long enough I will tell you where we are at & about our trip. We left home last Wedns. the 4th of Nov. & this is the 6 day on our journey. As a real norther blew up last eve, we are laying over in Jack Co., near the widow Estes place.

We traveled two days in the worst sand storms I ever saw—it is so dry we can't hardly get drinking water, much less stock water. As yet Mr. Turner hasn't over taken us yet, as he promised, but we are finding our way splendidly & we have had plenty company so far—only six wagons over taken us this side of Weatherford.

Pa mailed Dan a card at Whitt, yesterday morning asking him to meet us, (i.e., if he can get off) as we are heavy loaded—as yet we haven't traveled more than 18 miles in a day. If we ever do get to Matador, I hope we never make another long move like this. I am afraid Pa & Ma can't stand much exposure. It is over a days drive to Farmer. We will not go via Jacksboro, but will go via Seymour.

I had you two letters mailed last Tues. to Teepee City, doubt-less they have been forwarded to you by this time. I recd. a letter from you last Sat. & was glad you appreciated your [hair] chain. Maggie made it for me last spring while she was taking lessons in hair work. She has since given me lessons in the same accomplishment.

Oh! How I do wish we were at our destination. The wind is still blowing hard & cold. I will mail this to you at the first P. O., but don't know when that will be.

Pa has just come in from hunting water & he informs us we are about one mile from the widow Kieth's. I suppose she is a relation of yours. We are now on the Graham road & Mr. Jno. B. Estes is at home & is fraiting [freighting] on another road about 7 miles from this one. We are camped in a flat at the foot of a hill, where there is fine post oak timber. I hope to see you & Dan soon. As ever

Ella

Nov 18, 1891

(Postmark: Teepee City, Tex.)

To: Miss Ella Cribbs
Matador, Texas

From: Teepee City, Texas
Nov 17 1891

To: Miss Ella Cribbs

My dearest Girl. I take greate pleasure in answer your letter just recieved, though I was just fixing to write you a letter to Matador telling you whair I am. I am bourding at one off the farms, looking after some fence. When youal get to Matador, please write to me at Teepee City. So, I will come up as soon as I hear youal air thair.

I am so sorrow to know youal air having such disagreeable weather to travel in. I do trust youal will have prity weather from thair on. The way I have counted it up, I think youal will land at the end off your journir [journey] the 18th, that is tomorrow.

Yes, I recieved your last two leters. Well, I will close as tis getting late & I have six miles to go this earning & hope it will not be many days till we can see & talk with each other. So, I will close for this time. Good by, my Dear Girl & write as soon as you get this. Your truest friend.

D.C. Kieth

Nov 20, 1891

(Postmark: Matador Texas; a dove embossed on notepaper, writing in pencil, envelope smudged; on back of notepaper: "Pas glove no. 71.4, Collor light dove")

To: Mr. D.C. Kieth
Teepee City
Motley Co.) Texas

From: Matador Tex.
Nov 20 1891

To: D.C. Kieth

Dearest friend, Pa has just gave me your letter & I'll hastely ans. it as we are getting to go to the ball to night at Matador. I hope to meet you then. We didnt want to go one bit, but "Mrs. Mc" insist that we must go. We arrived here about this time yesterday evening—O.K.

*If I do not meet you at the bal,l I hope you will get this tomor-
row & come Sunday. Was sorry you was so badly disappointed
last Sun. I must close as the sun is nearly down. So by by. As ever*

Ella

Nov 2[3], 1891
(Postmark: Teepee City [Texas])

*To: Miss Ella Cribbs
Matador Texas*

*From: Teepee City Tex.
Nov 23 1891*

To: Miss Ella Cribbs

*My Dearest friend. I've just I your kind note this earning &
I am so glad to know youal landed safe. Hope your Father will get
the house fix up before it comes another cool spell. By the way, your
letter & a card from your Father is just hear & went to Childress
& back, So that iidn't I dident get them any sooner. I wish I could
come up at once, though I have a bout 4 days work to do down hear
& cant come at present with out letting my work go undon. So, I
will come next Friday or Saturday if possible. So good earning. I
remain your tru & faithful friend.*

D.C. Kieth

P. S. I send good wishes & respects

Dec 4, 1891
(Postmark: Teepee City Tex.)

To: Miss Ella Cribbs
Matador, Texas

From: Teepee City Texas
Dec 4 1891

To: Miss Ella Cribbs

My dear Girl, I take greate pleasure in writing you a few lines this earning. I hope this may find youal well. I am well at this time except a little coul and coff. I will start north in the morning to be gone a bout 3 or 4 days, if nothing hupons more than I am expecting.

I will come up thaire a bout the last off the week, I supose your Father is thaire by this time. I hope they returned safe. I will half to close, as I am in a littr hurrie. I hope you air injoying your self. So good by, my Dear Girl & write soon.

Your tru & loving friend

D.C. Kieth

Dec 14, 1891

(Postmark: Teepee City [Texas])

To: Miss Ella Cribbs
Matador, Texas

From: Teepee City Texas
Dec 13 1891

To: Miss Ella Cribbs

My Loving Girl. I take my pen in hand this rainy eave. to write to one who seames nearrer & dearrer than any one on earth to me. I believe it has only ben 2 days since I saw you, but seames more lik a week to me. The earning I left up thaire, I got home a bout dark, though I got prity coal as I was facing the wind & rain. This is such a good rain we air getting, if it will just quit without turning so coal & freezing.

If the weather dosent keep to bad, I will be up thair Wednesday on my way to north fens [fence], to fix up our litter home. Well, I expect this letter will close our pleasant correspondence wich has ben keep up so long. Oh, it has ben such a pleasant one to me. I will close hoping those few lines may find youal well. I am your tru & loving friend. As ever

D. Kieth

[Dec 18, 1891]

(No postmark; letter written on courthouse stationary;
note that Browning served as commissioner in 1891 only;
Precinct No. 1, Notary Public; Dan Browning, County
Commissioner, Motley County)

Dec 18 1891

To: Miss Ella Cribbs

My Dear Girl. I send you 2 pair of glovs, hoping one or the other will suit. The ones I have for my self is a red tan, though they air not the kind I sent for, but supose will do. So, no more at presant.

Your truest & faithfull friend,
D.C. Kieth
Good neight, my Dear Girl.

[Dec 21, 1891]

(No envelope)

From: Matador Tex.
Dec. 21 1891
To: Mr. D.C. Kieth

Dearest friend; I'll write you a few lines to let you know we are still at Mrs. Mc's. Unfortunately, we failed to get moved.

As you said you couldn't come back till Wedn., I'll just write this but am afraid you will not think to call for it. Mr. Mc. said it will be all right for us to be married here.

I recd. those things O.K. last Sat. evening.

As ever your

Ella

That's the last of the letters in the D.C. and Ella Cribbs Kieth Collection.

Motley County Museum, 804 Dundee St., Matador, Texas.

The Wedding
Motley County News
December 23, 1891
Wedding Announcement

"On this morning at 9 o'clock a.m. at the residence of Mrs. Mittie McDonalds, Mr. D.C. Keith [*sic*] to Miss Ella E. Cribbs, Esq. McHugh officiating . . . Mr. Walter A. Walton and Mr. H.L. White acting as groomsmen and the bride's lovely sisters, Miss Maggie and Miss Carrie Cribbs acting as bridesmaids. May their pathway be strewn with flowers and no sorrow ever be their lot is the best wishes of a friend."

The marriage took place at the McDonald Line Camp on the Matador Ranch in what became known as the McDonald Pasture, several miles south of the village of Matador. Much loved and appreciated by the ranch hands, Mrs. McDonald was included on the ranch payroll, doing laundry and cooking as needed. She took Ella under her protective wing as the Cribbs family relocated from Ft. Spunky near Granbury in Hood County. No further mention has been noted of Ella's reservation about Dee McDonald's character while he was living with his family near Ft. Spunky.

Sometime later Miss Carrie Cribbs married County Clerk Walter A Walton and Miss Maggie Cribbs married John Vaughn. Their brother Dan Cribbs quit the life of a cowboy and cotton farmer for one of adventure in the gold and copper fields before an untimely death at age 48.

The Original Letters

Included here are scanned images of a selection of the letters D.C. and Ella exchanged, to showcase the letters themselves and the handwriting of the period. Each of these letters has been retyped and can be more easily read in the previous section.

All of the letters in the Keith family collection have been retyped and are included in the earlier section, The Letters: Correspondence Between D.C. Kieth and Ella E. Cribbs, and are presented in chronological order. D.C. Kieth and Ella Cribbs wrote many more letters than have been saved.

December 12, 1886

[Written in brown ink on lined and folded writing paper, decorated with a flower in gray and green tones in the upper corner]

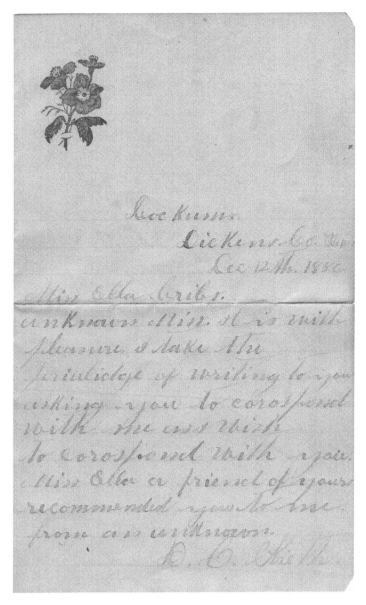

This was D.C.'s first letter to Ella and was the beginning of their five-year correspondence

Mar 18, 1887 Page 1

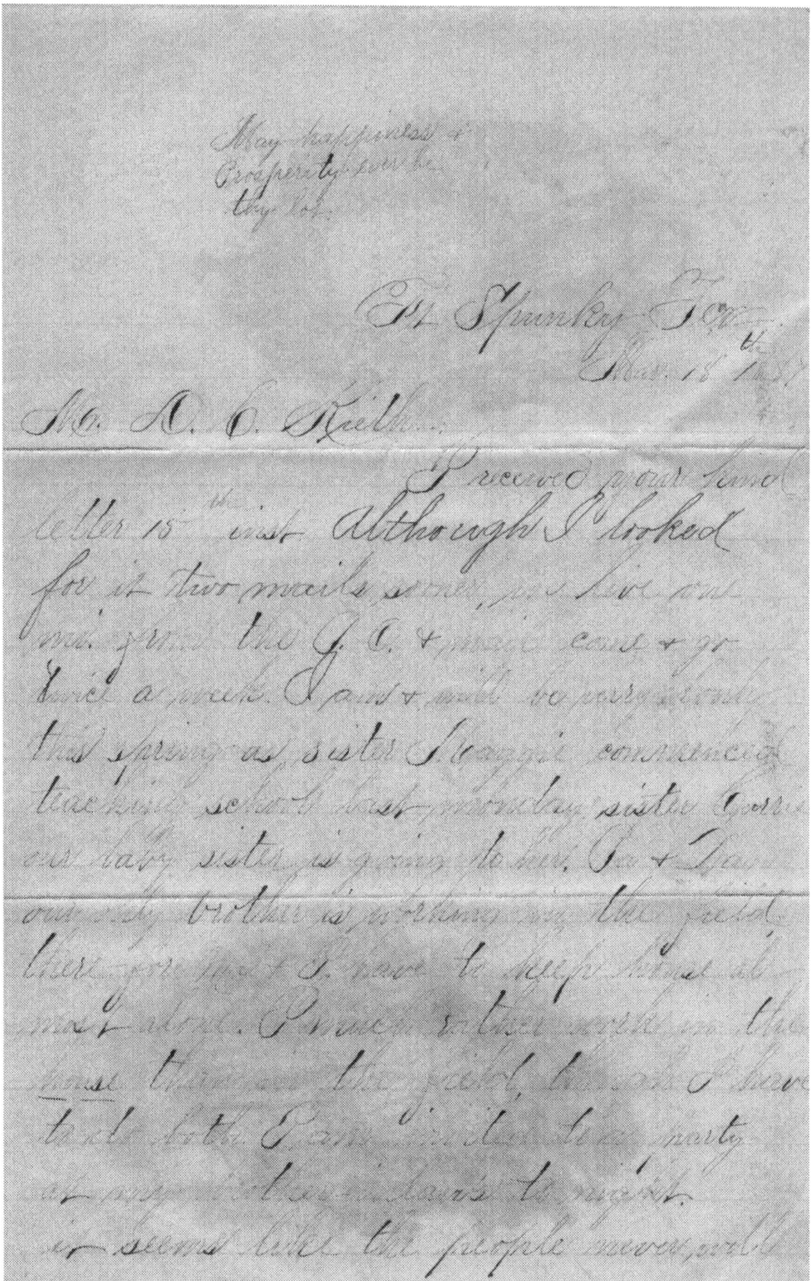

Mar 18, 1887 Page 2

yet tired of dancing. I dont dance,
though they never fail to send me
an invitation. I have not saw Miss
Myrounder since I wrote to you last.
She lives in a neighborhood about 7 miles
from ours.

I will send you one of my
pictures in my next letter, in exchange for one of yours. Believing
you will be as good as your word in
regard of returning it. As for taking
care of it I cant say it is worthy
of much protection.

You must plant a
garden or a melon patch for I will
make a good scarecrow to keep the
intruders off. Please excuse my
nonsense. You & your friend
Mr. Jenkins, must come down next
summer & enjoy the protracted
meetings and & other gatherings

Mar 18, 1887 Page 3

with me, as there is the
farmers holiday I believe
We also have Sunday school every sunday.
And a very interesting literary society
every Saturday night, night.

We have
had a good season since the if of
last June the if, for the farmers are
very much discouraged, & some have
left there homes & are gone to the
railroad. Do the people ever farm
any where you live & do is it very
seasonable out there?

Would it be asking to
much if you write me soon Please excuse
my inquisitiveness, & this written & composed
letter. Write soon & a long letter to your
faithful friend.

Ella Gibbs.

Mar 18, 1887 Page 4

Mar. 22, 1887 Page 1

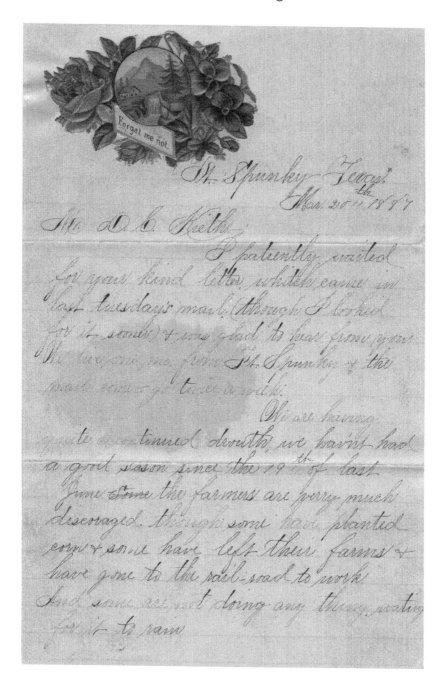

St. Spunky Texas
Mar 21th 1887

Mr. D. C. Keith,

I patiently waited
for your kind letter, which came in
last tuesday's mail (though I looked
for it sooner) & was glad to hear from you
We live one mi. from St. Spunky & the
mail comes up twice a week.

We are having
quite a continued drouth, we haven't had
a good season since the 19th of last
June. Some the farmers are verry much
discouraged. though some had planted
corn & some have left their farms &
have gone to the rail-road to work.
And some are not doing any thing waiting
for it to rain

Mar. 22, 1887 Page 2

Is it very reasonable in your part of the country, & is there any farms out there? I am & will be very busy this spring as sister Maggie commenced teaching school last monday. There is only 5 of us children. I have 2 sisters & one brother younger than myself. sister Maggie is the eldest. Now I have to keep house almost alone. I had much rather work in the house than in the field though I have done both. I attended a party at my brother-in-law's last friday night. I don't dance myself though we never fail to get an invitation.

I have not seen [Mr.......] since I wrote to you last. it is about 7 mi. from our neighborhood to where he lives. when I saw him he said he was going to start soon for the ranch. I will send you one of my pictures in my next in exchange for one of yours.

Mar. 22, 1887 Page 3

PS. Believing you will be as good as your word in regard of returning it. As for taking care of it, I can't say it is worthy of much protection.

You & your friend Mr. Perkins must come down next summer & enjoy the protracted meetings & other gatherings with us. As that is the farmers holiday I believe. We have sunday school every sunday morning & singing in the afternoon. & preaching three times a month. And we a very interesting spelling match every saturday night.

Would it be asking too much for your name in full, please excuse my inquisitiveness, & this badly written & composed letter. Write soon & a long letter to your faithful friend.

Ella Cribbs.

Mar [27], 1887 Page 1

Mar [27], 1887 Page 2

from any town.
you wanted to know if there
were a reasonable country
not carry it hasent rained
in this part of the country
for several months.
though I dont wonder at it
not raining in a cow country
for they work Sunday
as well as any other day
though it is most
imposible for a cow man
to tend to his bisness unless
he works on Sunday.
they is some few farms
in this countrie though
the most of them are nomd
farms raise mostly hay
for the horses ~~~~~~~
in the winter.
I dont think this countrie
will ever bee much of a

Mar [27], 1887 Page 3

farming countrie.
our friend Mr. Merriman
is in this countrie now
though I havent saw him
since he returned.
I havent saw Mr Jenkins
since last January I met
him one day on my line
and have spoke or talk
with him
are you acquainted
with Mr Jenkins
he dosent know that I am
corrospond with you
unless some one has
told him & think a great
of Mr. Jenkins he seems
to bee a verry nice young
man
Miss Ella I am sorrow
to think you will bee
so lonsom this Spring.

Mar [27], 1887 Page 4

I wish I could meet you
and talk with you
I think I would enjoy
my self with you.
you have no idea how
much I appreciate reading
your letters. If you should
fail to get an answer
from me to any of your
letters this summer
for some time you will
please not get offended
as I am liable to bee off
on a cow hunt and not
get your letter for
several days. I will close
for this time sending
my regards to you
write soon and oftin to you
know or not faithful friend

Daniel Crofford Keith

[August 9, 1887] Envelope

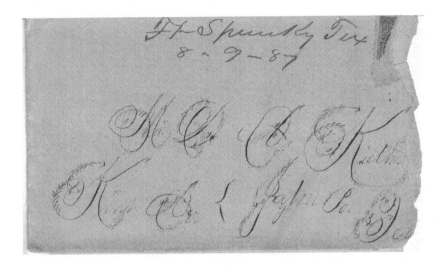

[August 9, 1887]

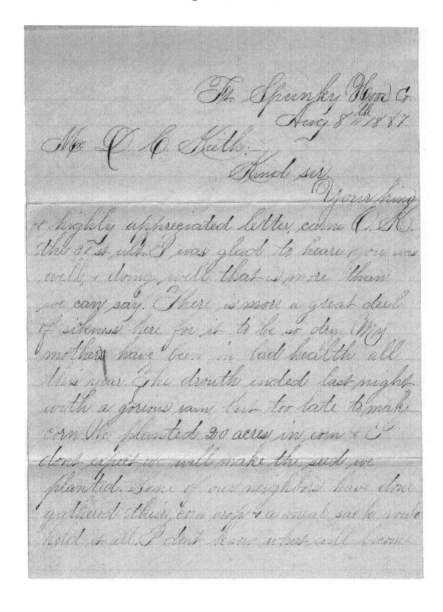

Feb 2, 1888 Longings Envelope

Feb 2, 1888 Longings

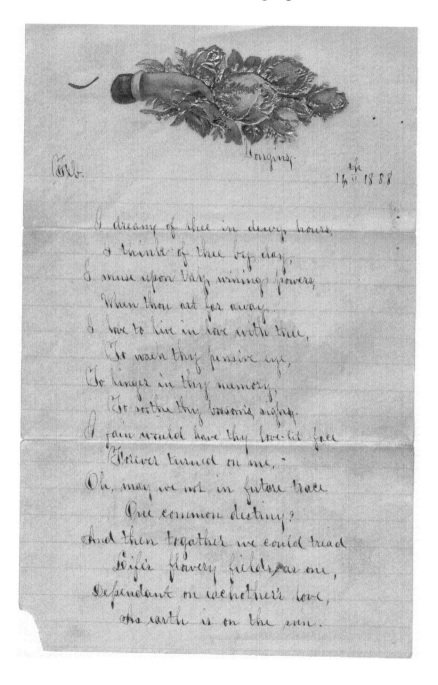

Feb.   *Longings.*   14th 1888

I dream of thee in dewy hours,
I think of thee by day,
I muse upon thy winning powers,
When thou art far away.
I love to live in love with thee,
To watch thy pensive eye,
To linger in thy memory,
To soothe thy bosom's sighs.
I fain would have thy love-lit face
Forever turned on me,—
Oh, may we not in future trace
One common destiny?
And then together we could tread
Life's flowery fields as one,
Dependant on eachother's love,
As earth is on the sun.

Feb 2, 1888 Longings Page 2

Each joy in life would brighter be,
If thou wert always near,
And every sorrow lighter be
If thou wert there to cheer,
So let me linger by thy side,
In love with thee alone,
Should ~~fortune frown or ills betide~~,
Thy presence would alone.
And blest and happy in thy smiles,
Despite of cross or care,
I'd pray for rare longevity
Thy holy love to share.

A Valentine from a
friend to a friend. —

Sep 3, 1888 Envelope

Sep 3, 1888 Page 1

1

Llockumr Texas
Sep 2rd 1888.
Miss Ella Cribbs
Absent friend,
I recieved your kind
& welcom letter to day.
I was glad to hear from
you. though was sorrow
to hear off your Sister,
being sick. I hope she
is well by this time.
I also hope this letter
will find youal well
& injoying your selves.
I am well though
I cant say I am injoying
my self verry much
though I dont think
I have eny wright to

Sep 3, 1888 Page 2

9

steamer to be lively & pleasent
& am sorrow to know you
aire married so eury day;
though & am glad to know
you rest so well at night.
& wish & was thaire to
joine your class this morning
though the class & will half
to joine from now on untill
a bout christmas will
be with the cows.
& will start on faul works
this eauning to be gone
seual days though & haue
no ida where & will be
at this Ranch a gain.
the Matalas Ranch will
be my head quarters
this faul.

Sep 3, 1888 Page 3

12

Matador Ranch
....

P.S. Received your letter &c

I also intend to have a
litter home & live at home
before many more years.
I mean that is my intention
weather I will them or not for
cirtain I cant say.
give Miss Maggie my
regards & tell his I hope
we all will live to see each
other. & I hope the time
isent fas off if your see
Mr M. give him my regards
I will close for this time
hoping to hear from youal
a gan soon your tru
& faithful friend untill
death.
D. E. Kieth
Good by.

April 12, 1889 Envelope

April 12, 1889

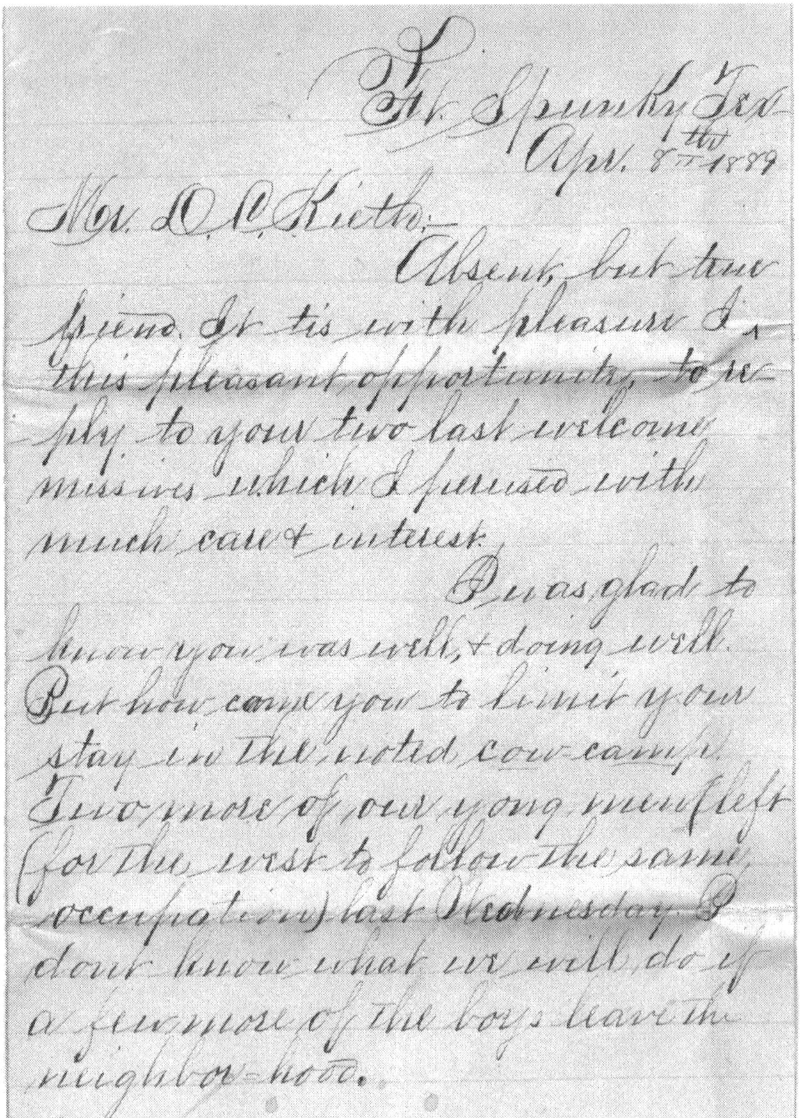

Ft. Spunky Tex
Apr. 8th 1889

Mr. D. C. Keith:—

Absent, but true friend. It tis with pleasure I this pleasant opportunity to reply to your two last welcome missives which I perused with much care & interest.

I was glad to know you was well, & doing well. But how came you to limit your stay in the noted cow-camp. Two more of our young men left (for the west to follow the same occupation) last Wednesday. I dont know what we will do if a few more of the boys leave the neighbor-hood.

Apr 18, 1890

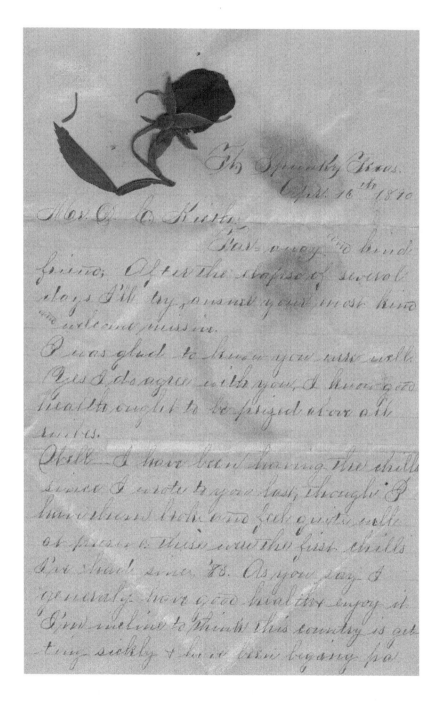

[Dec 15 1890] Envelope

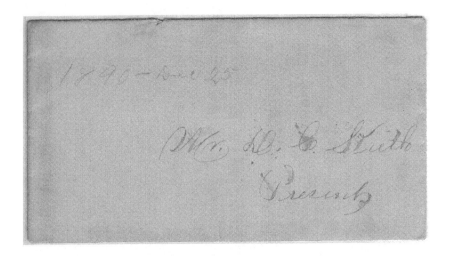

[Dec 15 1890]

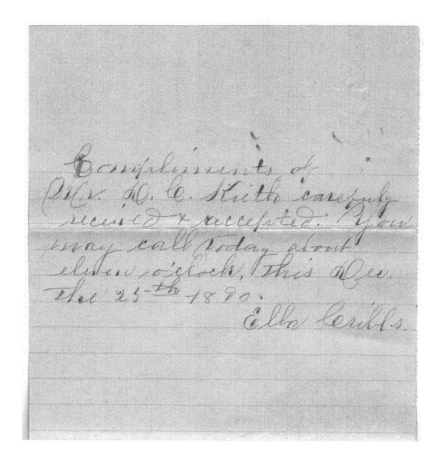

Compliments of
Rev. H. C. Keith carefully
received & accepted. You
may call today about
eleven o'clock, this Dec.
the 25th 1890.

Ella Cribbs.

Dec 31, 1890 Page 1

* OFFICE OF *

DEATON, KNOX & CO.,

Wholesale and Retail Grocers,

Stone Block, East Side of Swearingen Street.

Childress, Texas, *dec 30th* 1890.

Miss Ella Deribbr

Absent but two friend
it is with the greatest off pleasure
I write you a few lines to
night, I returned to this place
this evening with softly,
& have alredy met with
grate many off my warm
friends, dear johnie & I
seprated at ft Croorth this
morning a bout half past
nine oclock. I taken the train
for childress & they taken the
train for millsap. I believe
that was the place they
was going wasent it,
& also met two off my cow
boy friends at the fort & we

Dec 31, 1890 Page 2

* OFFICE OF *

DEATON, KNOX & CO.,

Wholesale and Retail Grocers,

Stone Block, East Side of Swearingen Street.

Childress, Texas,_____ 189 .

all came up to gether. they
had been down spending xmas
with relations in parker &
Tarant co, Well our holidays
air ones for a while nex thing
is work. & I can cirtainly go
to my work with a good &
wiling heart, for I can say my
xmas has been the most happiest
xmas to me for the past 10
years, an it is gitting late I will
half to close. please excuse paper
as the Po is closed & this kind
was all I could get to night.
please write at once & let me
know if youal returned hom
saft. I trust you did. love &
regards to youal. your tru friend
D. B. Ritta

good nuiwht

Feb 10, 1891 Envelope

Feb 10, 1891

OFFICE OF

County and District Clerk

CROSBY COUNTY

ATTACHED COUNTIES
DICKENS,   LUBBOCK
MOTLEY,   LYNN

SID. B. SWINK, Clerk.

Estacado, Texas, Feb 8th 1891

Miss Ella Scribber

My dear Friend

With great pleasure I write you a few lines this pleasant Sunday eve. Though I havent any reply from my last letter, but I think they will be a letter at the ranch for me from you when I return. I do trust they will come though I suppose I will get back to the ranch next Wednesday or Thursday. I landed at this place yesterday eve, three of us came up together in a hack, we came to Floid city the first day & had a dance [illegible] that night & also had a fine time. So they promised to give us another dance as we came back. by the way I went to church to day for the first time since I left Wood Co, it was a quakers meeting, & was the first one I was ever at. Most all these people are [illegible] in this town & believe are quakers & seeme to be very nice & clever, this is the oldest town I believe in northwest texas, our county was attached to this co, though we have a co

Postscript

Kieth/Keith Family Tree

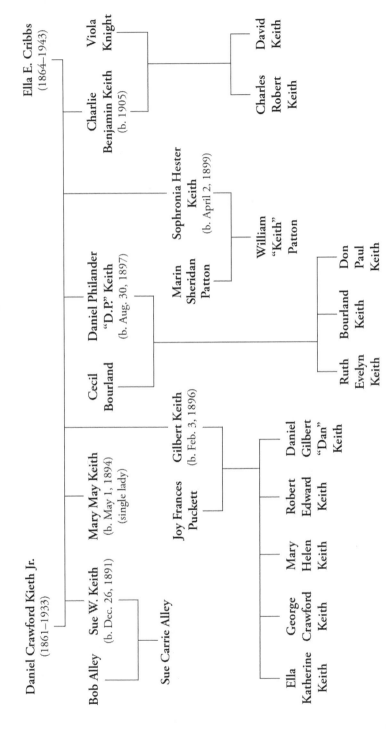

The Texas Tech Keiths in Print

Texas Techsan magazine, Vol. 50, No. 3, May/June 1997, pp. 22-25
Reprinted by Permission, 2022

Penpal Courtship Results in a Tech Legacy
By Marisue Burleson Potts

Nine grandchildren of D.C. and Ella Keith (Kieth), homesteaders in the Caprock foothills at the edge of the Llano Estacado, shared their family's common Western heritage. Another milestone these descendants of a cowboy and a cotton farmer's daughter share is their college alma mater, Texas Tech University of Lubbock, Texas. Their grandmother Ella's dream was always to become better educated, if only accomplished by going to school with younger students.

The Keith clan of Techsans include George Keith '52 of La Grange; Bob Keith '56 of Victoria; Dan Keith '62 of Shallowater; Bo Keith '55 of Albuquerque; Keith Patton '47 of Matador; Mary Helen Keith Knox '54, '82; Ruth Keith Latimer '47 and Don Keith '50, all of Lubbock; and Ella Katherine Keith Rowland '51, deceased.

In a parallel to the family odyssey, Keith Patton and his future bride, Joan Moyer, of Long Island, NY, became acquainted through a long-distance correspondence. As in the case of D.C. and Ella, the penpal romance of Keith and Joan culminated in their marriage in 1962, and they too settled in the small community of Matador on Keith land that was once the haunt of Comanches and buffalo hunters.

The year was 1880 when 19-year-old D.C. Keith helped his uncle trail a bunch of cattle to the wide open country of Dickens County. Near their campsite at Soldier's Mound, the rolling plans were dotted with herds of wild mustang and antelope, but only a few buffalo remained. A smattering of renegade Indians caused little concern to the 28 residents rustled up for the census. The country appealed to the Tennessee farm boy's sense of adventure, and two years later he was back to stay, as a "cow boy" on Dockum's Ranch.

The cowboy's life was lonely; his routine of cow hunts boring and certainly lacking in female companionship. So Keith quizzed a friend about likely candidates and came up with the name of a young lady back in the Brazos River bottomland of Hood County. But Miss Ella Cribbs was none too interested in corresponding with one of those wild cowboys. Keith assured her that cowboys weren't half as wild as their reputations.

The story of their correspondence and subsequent romance, which covers five years from 1886 to 1891, is documented in a series of 85 letters saved in a shoebox tied with twine. From the stained parchment of one letter fell a dark red rose, pressed and preserved for more than 100 years.

The letters detail the diverse lives of the two: the ranching frontier, on one hand, and the farming frontier, on the other. The busy cotton farmer's daughter, who cared for her ailing mother, cooked and took care of the household chores, hardly had time to write the lonely fellow. When she did write, her hands were often sore from picking in the "detestable old cotton patch." Miss Ella managed to pick 6,000 pounds of cotton by late November 1888, but she lamented that her father planned to plant a "really big crop" the following year.

Searching for better benefits as a ranch worker, Keith first joined the Espuela Co., and then the TO Ranch, which let him run his string of cattle along with the ranch's herd. When that didn't work out he returned to the Espuela.

In one letter he berated his friend for thinking of herself as an old maid at age 22, and then made her a proposal: "How would you like to keep house in the west for a cowboy?"

After a huffy brush-off, he confided to her that he had made up his mind to marry when he reached 30, provided he lived that long. Death was often on his mind as he pursued cow hunts, pushed unruly herds to the railheads, fought prairie fires and camped out in the unpredictable weather.

When Keith once again asked for a description of his penpal, he offered one of himself. "My eyes air gray. I am high tempered and I drink whiskey, though I can controle myself. I am stout and healthy and have been all my life."

Figuring he had told her the worst, he once again popped the question. "Miss Ella, do you believe you can think enough of me to promis me your hand & heart in matrimonia?" He advised her to direct her letters to the Matador Ranch, an outfit that promised "a little better" wages.

Keith finally wrangled time off from his ranchhand chores, and after much parleying back and forth, he boarded the train to visit Miss Ella. On Christmas Day 1890, he called on her at the family home near Fort Spunky. For the very first time, after years of corresponding, they met face to face. The six-day visit went well and a wedding date was set before he left for cattle shipping points in Childress; Degraff, Kan.; Fort Madison, Iowa; and Chicago. His letters reveal he looked forward to becoming a homesteader and building a house.

Ella's father became determined to leave the droughty cotton farm to relocate to Keith's country. As they made preparations to leave Hood County, Keith was off mustanging.

"I had ben running a bunch of wild horses all day & was very tired." From the railhead where they had trailed 1,700 head of cattle, Keith licked his stubby pencil and wrote, "The Boys has all gone to bed except myself and 2 that is on first gard. I am siting by my lantern trying to write to one who seams so dear to me."

Ella's family, on their wagon trip from Fort Spunky, faced a blue norther and sand storms, a shortage of stock water and an overloaded wagon. But, in contrast, upon arrival in Motley County they were immediately invited to a ball. Miss Cribbs engaged a dressmaker to create a two-piece basque wedding dress of gray cashmere and velvet, trimmed with 24 steel buttons.

Ella Cribbs and D.C. Keith ended their long-distance romance on Dec. 23, 1891, and began their marriage which resulted in six children: Sue, Mary, Charlie, D.P., Helen and Gilbert. From the children of D.P., Helen and Gilbert come the nine Keith cousins who graduated from Texas Tech.

During his years at Tech, **George Keith '52** worked in the Department of Animal Science with Dean W.L. Stengel and held the position as beef cattle herdsman. After graduation, he held a similar position with Pantex Farms and the Texas A&M bull testing program. He held positions with Nutrena as salesman, Giddings as profit center manager, and Cargill as district manager.

After he took early retirement from Cargill in La Grange, George worked in radio sales and served as manager of a radio station, a natural for him. Not only had he taken radio speech classes at Tech, but in 1953 he hosted Sunday afternoon television broadcasts with live demonstrations provided by local 4H and FFA chapters. After his second retirement at age 62, George began transporting automobiles for local dealerships.

George and his wife, Leona Sagebiel Keith '70, who is a retired school teacher, met during their college days at the Tech Rec Center and were wed six months later. They are the parents of Diane, Sheila Prause '81 and Dee McIlroy '82.

Texas Tech's cooperative living program at Casa Linda made it possible for **Ella Katherine Keith Rowland '51** and her sister **Mary Helen Keith Knox '54** to attend college. At Casa Linda 18 girls shared household, management and supervision duties in a two-story house on campus, a venture that made college affordable, especially for women from rural farm families experiencing the droughty '50s. According to Mary Helen, Dean Margaret Weeks, head of the home economics school, just could not keep the sisters straight or call them by their correct names.

Ella Katherine majored in home economics education and taught at Paint Rock, Stamford and Anson and earned a master's degree in testing and counseling. She and her husband, Brad Rowland, became the parents of Keith, Lynn '76, Richard and Mary. Ella Katherine passed away in 1983 at the age of 53.

Mary Helen recently retired from teaching after 30 years at Cooper ISBD in Lubbock County, where she had taught fifth through seventh grades. Over the years she applied what she learned at Tech in her major of home economics, raised her kids and taught a lot of others. In 1982 she returned to school to earn her master's degree in education supervision. Mary Helen, who is proud of her work with the gifted and talented program, served two years as assistant principal before becoming elementary school curriculum director.

"There's nothing more exciting than to see a child learn," she said. Although now retired, she continues to use her nurturing skills as caregiver of her family and looks forward to spending time as a part-time reading therapist. Mary Helen and her husband, Jack, a retired greenhouse operator, are the parents of Jerry '75, Danny '74, John Jay and Judy Knox Briggs '86.

A registered professional engineer, **Bob Keith '56,** who lives in Victoria, majored in electrical engineering and participated in the Air Force ROTC program. After graduation he worked briefly for DuPont in Orange, Texas, before going into the Air Force for three years. He then returned to DuPont in Orange before going into the Air Force for three years. He then returned to DuPont as an instrument engineer and held several supervisory positions. He transferred to Victoria in 1969 and then to Wilmington, Del., in 1973 as project manager for a new high-density polyethylene plant to be built in Victoria. Bob returned to Victoria in 1974 and held the positions of mechanical superintendent, engineering manager and senior consultant.

When Bob retired from Dupont in 1993, he began a consulting business which was involved in public affairs, environmental and management issues. He represents Victoria County in controversial surface-groundwater rights and in water interests related to the Edwards Aquifer. He and his wife, Doreta, are active in community and church activities. He has served as chairman of the Chamber of Commerce. They are the parents of Rhonda Keith Vanderpool, Randall, Stanley, and Stacy.

Ruth Keith Latimer '47 recalls one of the highlights of her days on the Tech campus was living in the Home Management House where she and other coeds worked in a home setting and rotated all the household responsibilities, including caring for a baby. Since nobody had a car, she and friends often walked to the Carnation ice cream parlor on Ave. Q for a weekend treat of sandwiches and hot fudge sundaes. Ruth lived in both Doak Hall and the newest dorm, Craddock, later known as Drane, where discipline was strict.

"Girls coming in late had to rouse a counselor. They were charged a late fee and required to appear before the dorm house senate," she said.

During her senior year, on a trip home to Matador, Ruth struck up an acquaintance with Lloyd Latimer at the Phillips 66 station. A few months later they were married in Matador, where Lloyd operated the station and she taught home economics. Like her grandmother, Ella Cribbs, Ruth felt the sting of disappointment when the drought made their attempts at dryland farming go awry. The Latimers moved to Lubbock where they continue to make their home. When the youngest of three children started school, Ruth returned to teaching for 10 years, while Lloyd, who retired in 1983, put in more than 27 years at the post office. The coupled celebrated their 50th wedding anniversary in February [1997]. They are the parents of Sandy Latimer Rowlett, Dale '76, and Kelly '79.

Don Paul Keith '50 a retired geologist, entered Tech in 1944, but left to serve in the Navy from 1945 to 1946. When he re-entered college in 1946, he was a member of the Wrangler fraternity and the Air Force ROTC program. Upon graduation with a BS degree in geology, he served two additional years in the Air Force. He and Frances Breedlove were married while he was stationed in Sherman. They later adopted a son, Larry, and twin girls, Charlotte and Carrie.

For more than 32 years Don Paul worked as an exploration geologist for Atlantic Richfield Corp. in Houston and Corpus Christi, retiring in 1985. Widowed in 1990, Don Paul later married Jean James, and they now call Lubbock home. However, they spend much of the year traveling and have just returned from a very special trip to the Holy Land.

[paragraph omitted]

Bourland "Bodie" Keith '55, of Albuquerque, received his BS in mechanical engineering. After attending graduate school at the University of Texas, he worked with the Air Force at Alamogordo, then transferred to the Navy Missile Test Facility at White Sands Missile Range. As missile flight test engineer he set parameters for launching sounding rockets, high altitude test rockets, and for flight tests of the TALOS Navy shipboard missiles.

In 1960 he transferred to Kirtland Air Force Base in Albuquerque to the Naval Weapons Evaluation Facility to conduct tests and studies of Navy shipboard nuclear missiles. Though he retired in 1990, he and his wife, Nancy, are active in church work in Albuquerque, Habitat for

Humanity, and Project Share, a project for feeding the homeless. Yet, the Albuquerque couple still finds time to play tennis and enjoy the slopes in both downhill and cross country skiing in the Sandias and mountains of New Mexico. Bodie's children are Peter and Wendy.

When **Dan Keith '62** attended Tech, he worked for his father, Gilbert, on their farm at Whiteface. Because Dan drove to Lubbock to attend classes, his on-campus activities were somewhat limited. When he graduated with a degree in animal science, he put his knowledge and background in the College of Agriculture to work by becoming a farmer. In addition, for three years he served as judge for Cochran County. Dan became involved in municipal work and is currently the director of public utilities for the City of Shallowater. He and his wife, Sandra Dickson Keith '84, are the parents of Valerie Keith Taylor, Gary, David '86, '88, Pam and Steven.

Recently, Dan and Sandra made a trip to Georgetown at the request of their grandson, Andrew Taylor. The young Williams Elementary School student wanted his class to hear about cowboys, Keith style. So Dan hauled out the dutch ovens his father, Gilbert, used to heat up around the chuck-wagons on the Matador Land & Cattle Co.'s range in the counties of Motley, Floyd, Dickens, and Cottle. He lugged them down-country and made sourdough biscuits for the class. Dan also shared with the students a video taken at Lubbock's Ranching Heritage Center wherein stands the relocated Matador Ranch dugout, a crude but comfortable subterranean dwelling where Gilbert and more than a few rattlesnakes had bunked upon occasion.

And Dan Keith, while playing the part of a chuckwagon coosie, told them the sweet story of a cowboy and a cotton farmer's daughter, a first-rate, long-distance romance of the Old West.

When **Keith Patton '47** entered Texas Tech he was 17 and only two years older than the young college. He recalled that he lived in the dorm.

"In fact," he said, I lived in both of the men's dorms, at different times. There were only two on campus."

Patton interrupted his college career with three years in the Army Air Force serving with the First AACS Wing. Upon his return to Tech, he graduated with Honors in history. After attending graduate school at UT, he became a schoolteacher for a few years. Then, like his Keith grandparents, he made Motley County his home and became a farmer-stockman on the land his grandfather homesteaded in 1890.

Kieth/Keith Family Timeline

1834 – Daniel Crawford Kieth Sr. born on 30 January 1834, to Elizabeth Miller and Porter James Kieth. Siblings are Elizabeth [Eleanor], Susan, John Ross, and George Jones Kieth.

1854 – Daniel Crawford Kieth Sr. married Susan C. Bledsoe, 27 August 1854, in Franklin County, Tennessee.

1855 – Daniel Sr. and wife, Susan, were in Parker County, Texas, where daughter Sophronia was born on 6 October 1855. Frequent Indian attacks in the area discouraged them from staying in Texas and they returned to Tennessee.

1860 – Census of Franklin, Tennessee, lists Daniel Sr., age 26; Susan, 25; Sophronia E., 4; and Charles Bledsoe, 1.

1861 – Daniel Sr. enlisted in April with Turney's 1st Tennessee Infantry at Winchester, Tennessee. The unit marched through the Cumberland Gap to Winchester, Virginia, to a very crowded Camp Jones.

On 8 July 1861, Daniel Sr. wrote a poignant letter to his children, fearing he would not survive to return to his family. One month later, on 8 August 1861, he died of pneumonia after a relapse of the measles. His name is listed in the Winchester National Cemetery, but his gravesite is unknown. Baby boy D.C., named for his father, was born on 7 October 1861 in Tennessee.

1877 – Isom Linn, husband of Daniel Sr.'s sister, Mary Eleanor Jane Keith (b. 22 February 1842, d. 18 December 1881), left Jack County, Texas, for Dickens County, Texas.

1880 – D.C. Kieth Jr., 19, was enumerated in District 12, Franklin, Tennessee, living with his uncle, A.S. Bledsoe, farmer, and family. He and two other young men listed their occupations as servants on the 1880 census, Tennessee.

His Texas-born sister, Sophronia, and her husband, Henry Zachery Taylor Garner, took D.C. with them when they moved to Jack County, Texas. D.C. joined his uncle, Jones Kieth, in a cattle drive to Dickens County.

1882 – D.C. returned to Dickens County where he found work at Dockum's Ranch and other ranches.

1885 – Working as a cowboy, D.C. asked a friend for the name of a possible pen pal, and D.C. wrote for the first time to Ella Cribbs.

1890 – D.C. accompanied H.H. Campbell to Estacado to petition for the organization of Motley County.

1891 – Cribbs family moved to Motley County, and one month later, Ella and D.C. were married on 23 December 1891, at McDonald Camp. They moved into a dugout on the North Pease River for the Matador Ranch.

1900 – Census listed Danial [Daniel] Keith [note changed family name spelling], 38, b. 1861, at home in Precinct 4, Motley County, white, male, head of household of Ella E. and children from 7 to 1 years: Susan, Mary, Gilbert, Daniel, Sophie.

1907 – The Kieth family left their improved dugout and moved to their home, south of Matador.

1910 – Census listed Daniel C. Keith, 48, home in Precinct I, Motley County, married to Ella E. Keith, living with five of their children: Mary, 15; Gilbert, 14; D.P., 12; Hester, 10; and Charley [Charlie], 5.

Cribbs Family Timeline

1773 – 24 August, Peter Cribbs, Pennsylvania, was listed as a passenger on ship of unknown destination.

1800 – 18 May, Daniel Cribbs was born, son of Peter.

1811 – 6 January, Amy Lavery was born, daughter of Peter (d. 25 August 1883).

1829 – Daniel Cribbs opened a jug factory, two miles south of Tuscaloosa, Alabama.

1830 – Daniel Cribbs, listed in Indiana County, Pennsylvania.

1840 – Daniel Cribbs, listed in Indiana County, Pennsylvania, Blackwick Township.

1850 – Alabama census, Tuscaloosa, County, lists children of Daniel Cribbs: Anna (Amy Lavergy) Cribbs, Phylander [sic] Cribbs, 14, Lucinda Lavergy, 52.

1852 – California census, Placer County, lists Philander Cribbs, 16, miner, born Alabama, last residence, Alabama. Also Daniel Cribbs, 50, trader, born Pennsylvania, last residence

Alabama; Emma [Anna or Amy?], 43, born New York, last residence Alabama; Adaline Cribbs, 21, born Alabama, last residence Alabama.

1859 – Nannie Gertrude McShann answered letters from Philander "Phi" Cribbs with datelines of Sweet Home, Union, and Greene County, Alabama. "The Angels twine for thee a wreath of immortality."

1860 – Philander Cribbs, 25, living with brother Harvey.

1870 – U.S. census, Texas: home Precinct 1, Young County, Texas. Philander Cribbs, 43; Nanny G. Cribbs, 38, born Alabama, her parents' birthplaces, Kentucky; Ella E., 14, and other children.

Bibliography

Allen, Ruth. *The Labor of Women & Production of Cotton*. Austin: University of Texas, Bulletin #3134, 8 Sept. 1931.

Collinson, Frank. *Life in the Saddle*. Norman: University of Oklahoma, 1963.

Campbell, Harry H. *The Early History of Motley County*. Wichita Falls, Texas: Nortex, 1971.

Dickens County History. Spur, Texas: Dickens County Historical Commission, 1986.

Cribbs, Ella. Letters of D.C. and Ella Cribbs Kieth. Keith Family Collection, Motley County Historical Museum, Matador, Texas.

Farmers Alliance Records, 1887-1896. Micro H 776 Hood County Southwest Collection, Texas Tech University, Lubbock, Texas.

Friedberger, Mark. *The History of Ranching in North America*. Class notes by Marisue Potts, Spring Semester, 1995, Texas Tech University.

Green, Duff. *Recollections*. Mineral Wells, Texas: Joan Green Lawrence, 1998. Motley County Museum, Matador, Texas.

Walter Prescott Webb, ed. *Handbook of Texas*, Vol. I. Austin: Texas State Historical Assn., 1952.

Holden, W.C. *The Espuela Land & Cattle Company*. Austin: Texas State Historical Assn., 1970.

Kelton, Emer. *The Day the Cowboys Quit*. Ft. Worth: Texas Christian Press, 1971.

Kieth, D.C. Letters of D.C. and Ella Cribbs Kieth. Keith Family Collection, Motley County Historical Museum, Matador, Texas.

Pearce, W.M. *The Matador Land and Cattle Company*. Norman: University of Oklahoma, 1964.

Potts, Marisue Burleson. *Motley County Roundup: Over 100 Years of Gathering* (Floydada, Texas: Marisue Potts, 1991; Matador, Texas: Mollie Burleson Ranch Ltd., 2020, Second Edition).

Stafford, W.R. Espuela Ranch Files. Oral history abstract concerning W.C. Dockum, 29 Nov. 1929. Southwest Collection, Texas Tech University, Lubbock, Texas.

Traweek, Eleanor. *Of Such as These: A History of Motley County, Texas*. Quanah, Texas: Nortex, 1973.

Wallace, Ernest, and Adam Hoebel. *The Comanches: Lords of the South Plains*. Norman, Oklahoma: University of Oklahoma, 1952.

About the Author

Born in Matador, Texas, Marisue Burleson Potts grew up on a ranch where her father and grandfather ran herds of Hereford cattle. A 1960 graduate of Floydada High School in Floydada, Texas, she graduated from Texas Tech University in 1998 after the last of her five children had graduated from the same Lubbock institution.

She has served as Motley County Historical Commission chairman and a founding board member of the Motley County Historical Museum, Matador; the Comanchero Canyons Museum, Quitaque, Texas; and the Canyonlands Archeological Society of

Quitaque and Matador. During 2012-2013, she served as president of the West Texas Historical Association of Lubbock, Texas, and has made presentations of a historical nature at their annual conferences, as well as other heritage organizations. Her articles have been published in the *Matador Tribune,* the *Motley County Tribune,* the *Valley Tribune,* the *Caprock Courier,* the *Texas Techsan* magazine, the *Lubbock Avalanche Journal,* and the National Cowboy Symposium's *The Catch-Pen: A Selection of Essays from the First Two Years of the National Cowboy Symposium and Celebration.*

Marisue is the author of *Motley County Roundup: Over 100 Years of Gathering in Texas* (Mollie Burleson Ranch Ltd., 2020), *Ridgely Greathouse: Confederate, Conspirator, Convict, and Capitalist* (Mollie Burleson Ranch Ltd., 2021), and *Cowgirls Don't Cry: A Personal Reflection on a Life Shaped by the Pease River Breaks* (Mollie Burleson Ranch Ltd., 2021).

Index

Made in the USA
Columbia, SC
13 August 2024

39890455R00183